ALSO BY PAUL E. JOHNSON

Sam Patch, the Famous Jumper

The Kingdom of Matthias:
A Story of Sex and Salvation in 19th-Century America
(with Sean Wilentz)

A SHOPKEEPER'S MILLENNIUM

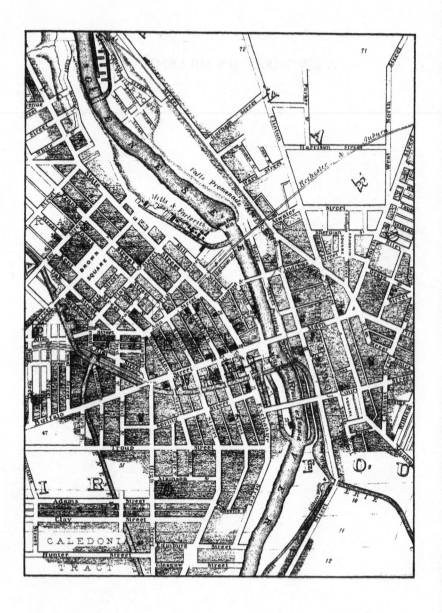

A
SHOPKEEPER'S
MILLENNIUM

SOCIETY AND REVIVALS IN
ROCHESTER, NEW YORK
1815–1837

Paul E. Johnson

Hill and Wang · New York

A division of Farrar, Straus and Giroux

Hill and Wang
A division of Farrar, Straus and Giroux
18 West 18th Street, New York 10011

Printed in the United States of America
First edition published in December 1978 by Hill and Wang
First revised edition, 2004

Library of Congress Control Number: 2004103268
ISBN: 0-8090-1635-4
EAN: 978-0-8090-1635-8

Designed by Nancy Dale Muldoon

www.fsgbooks.com

20 19

FOR MARCIA

Contents

List of Tables   ix
List of Maps   xi
Preface to the 25th-Anniversary Edition   xiii

INTRODUCTION   3
1. ECONOMY   15
2. SOCIETY   37
3. POLITICS   62
4. IMPASSE   79
5. PENTECOST   95
6. CHRISTIAN SOLDIERS   116
   AFTERWORD   136

Appendix A: Occupational Groups   142
Appendix B: Rochester Church Records   152
Notes   162
Acknowledgments   205
Index   209

Tables

1. Church membership and persistence, 1830–34   34

2. Partnerships formed by churchgoers and non-churchgoers, 1821–29   35

3. Church membership and occupation, 1825–31   103

4. Church membership among selected proprietors, 1827–34   104

5. Church membership and household composition, 1827   106

6. Changes in household composition, 1827–30   107

7. Distribution of occupations within assessment deciles, 1827   143

8. Households headed by skilled workmen, 1827   145

9. Manufacturers in assessment deciles 1 through 5, 1827   147

10. The Evangelical Churches of Rochester, 1815–38   157

11. Annual turnover in three congregations   159

12. Church membership and listings in city directories   160

13. Occupations and method of admission in two churches   161

Maps

Rochester in 1838   ii

Rochester Neighborhoods in 1827   49

Rochester Neighborhoods in 1834   50

Preface to the 25th-Anniversary Edition

JUDGED by the life expectancy of history books, *A Shopkeeper's Millennium* should have been dead long ago. Yet it remains a mainstay of courses in American history: it moves toward 100,000 copies in print, and a Web search turns up a small mountain of course syllabi, study guides, Web modules, and used copies—along with four sites at which one may purchase a student essay on *A Shopkeeper's Millennium*. (My favorite among these is www.cheathouse.com.) The book has, however, sustained a lot of criticism. A new edition presents an opportunity to survey a quarter-century's worth of criticism and new scholarly directions, and to tell new and old readers what I think is right and wrong about this book.

In 1978 *A Shopkeeper's Millennium* was part of the "new social history." Historians of my generation did not want to write about kings and wars. Our subject was the "inarticulate" ordinary Americans who formed the "base" of American society, but who left only a faint and scattered paper trail. We all looked for ways of giving voice to these voiceless Americans, and some of us placed great faith in quantifiable evidence. We read British and American structuralist sociological studies of social mobility, family structure, and so on, and some of us read the classics of Marx, Durkheim, and Weber as well. We determined to phrase historical questions as "hypotheses," then locate and "operationalize" our "data," count it up, and publish our "findings." The result, we promised, would be history "from the bottom up"—history grounded in the "social structures" and "patterns of action" that underlie the elitist froth of politics and high culture.

A Shopkeeper's Millennium was a part of that. It was addressed most explicitly to Lee Benson, whose *Concept of Jacksonian Democracy* (1961) "scientifically" demonstrated that ethnic and cultural divisions shaped the beginnings of two-party politics in the North more decisively than did questions of social class. In particular, Benson (he and his followers were quickly named "ethnoculturalists") found that an activist evangelical Protestantism was at the heart of the Whig Party in New York State. My own reading convinced me that Benson was right. But evangelical politics was new in the 1830s. I wanted to "test" whether it was the result of cultural inheritance or of the well-known revivals of the 1820s and 1830s. These revivals sustained new popular theologies, new personalities, new domestic forms, new notions of the good society, and a spate of new religious and reform organizations—the northern Whig Party, I suspected, among them. It seemed possible that all of this might have something to do with the making of a middle class, perhaps even with the economic and cultural transformations that historians now call the market revolution. My question was simple: A lot came out of these revivals, but what went into them? In 1978, only a "systematic social analysis" could provide an answer.

Western New York was a center of both the religious and the social transformations, and I decided to make Charles Finney's revival at Rochester in 1830–31 my "case study." So I drove my old Volkswagen bus from California to Rochester and camped in the neighborhood. (Webster Park, near Lake Ontario, was a favorite.) I went into Rochester, found old church records, and wrote down the names of members and their dates of admission. The city directories of 1827, 1834, and 1838 listed occupations and addresses at three points in time. Tax lists from 1827, 1830, and 1837 provided the assessed valuations of real and personal property held by individuals in those years. And the index to newspapers at the Rochester Public Library recorded some of the political and reform activities of the people I was studying. The result was a tall stack of half-sheets, each bearing a name and a statistical "biography." (I also read newspapers and manuscript diaries and letters, but these were suspect "literary" sources, left by a tiny and "unrepresentative" elite, and I did not count on getting much from them.)

At the time, my approach was achingly up-to-date. *A Shopkeeper's Millennium* was a "systematic test" of the hypothesis proposed by the ethnoculturalists. It was a quantitative "community study"—an attempt to explain religious change through intensive local analysis. Better yet, it was "holistic," comprehending social, economic, political, and religious changes all at once—or at least as a sequence of quantified moments. It was by analyzing those moments, I promised, that I would locate the "causes" of religious revivals in a "systematic" way. I was, in 1978, a believer. How else could I have written this: "With these methods we can demonstrate ways in which various changes intersected in the lives of persons who joined churches during revivals, and thus define the specific social strains that underlay the rise of evangelicalism. We can, in short, systematically trace the social origins of revival religion."

The result was a book that traced Rochester's middle-class revivals (and thus the local Whig electorate) to problems of legitimacy and moral order that attended the making of modern work. More broadly, the revival was bound up with the making of a middle-class culture within the transformations of the market revolution. I concluded that Benson's principal ethnocultural division had its historical roots in the rise of modern social classes. At the time, it was a slick piece of work.

Much of this way of doing history is over with now. Social science and quantification did not open up a new direction for history. In retrospect, they were something like the last gasp of positivism. (In the paragraphs that you have read, the words and phrases in quotation marks will strike twenty-first-century readers as quaint. That is because they are parts of a dead vocabulary.) This book survives as an undergraduate text because undergraduates continue to learn from it and to enjoy reading it, but in graduate seminars it survives largely as an example of where social science history went wrong. Many graduate students have cut their critical teeth on this book, and over the years their criticisms have accumulated into a three-part indictment: my crimes against theory and method, my crimes against religion, and my crimes against women.

A Shopkeeper's Millennium explains religious revivals in terms of social change, and it has been attacked as "reductionist": it reduces religion to something else. (In recent years, this has become "reflectionist.") Some critics have insisted that religious experience cannot be talked about in nonreligious terms, and any religious person knows the fundamental truth of that. Yet the same person, if he or she is a historian, must acknowledge that religious experiences and traditions wax and wane and change over time, that they often change in ways that are clearly a part of history, and that they are therefore proper subjects for historians of society and culture. The newer historians of culture acknowledge this much, but argue that economic, domestic, social, and religious experiences (categories that are themselves artificial abstractions) change in constellation, and that within any given constellation it makes no sense to look for "causes." Historians now like to study the ways in which experience is shaped by (and into) culture—and even argue that all history worth studying *is* culture.

I agree with some of that, and I certainly admit that talk of base and superstructure (or, in the case of this book, the attempt to specify the social causes of a religious revival) is a dubious business. I have not made such efforts in my more recent work. But I remain convinced of the existence of hard social reality—including the world of work, inequality, and social class—and of the necessity of including that reality in social and cultural history. The alternative, in the case of this book, would be to talk about the rise of the American middle class and its religion without mentioning class—with no other classes, no structured inequality, no market revolution, nothing of what we used to call history—nothing but middle-class psyches, feelings, imaginations, and interior decoration. Too much recent scholarly literature has chosen that alternative.

Other critics of method have worried about the evidence itself: the surviving church records were incomplete and came principally from the more prosperous churches; many church members (nearly all women and a large proportion of men) did not appear in tax lists, city directories, and other sources, and thus were absent from all but a few calculations; the dates of religious conversion, tax assessments, city directories, and censuses seldom matched, and "biographies" made from them were necessarily fuzzy and incomplete. A continuous history based in snapshots made from such evidence is inherently suspect.

Finally and most important, some of the more detailed calculations included too few cases to yield meaningful statistical results. (As many quantitative historians discovered, this tends to happen when the questions become detailed enough to be interesting.) That is particularly true of the explanatory section that begins on page 102. Key points of that and subsequent sections—the hard-edged language about social control in particular—should have been presented more modestly and with greater caution. (On a recent visit to the University of Rochester, I was shown the late Christopher Lasch's copy of *A Shopkeeper's Millennium*. At one point, he wrote in the margin: "We could use a little more delicate instrument here." Professor Lasch was evidently a nice man—certainly one who knew the value of understatement.)

Next, my crimes against religion. In 1978 American religious history centered on the Puritans and their descendants.

The Whig-reformist evangelical tradition that I was trying to explain clearly traced back to Puritanism, and it centered in New England and in Yankee colonies (like Rochester) farther west. In the case of Rochester, the post-Puritan emphasis was reinforced by the survival of church records: Presbyterian records were nearly complete (as were those of the Episcopalians), while Baptists and, particularly, Methodists were severely under-represented in the available records. Appendix B measures the probable results: the available records are weighted heavily toward the comfortable New Englanders who sat at the top of Rochester society.

American religious history has gotten bigger over the past twenty-five years. A number of fine studies have demonstrated the variety and magnitude of nineteenth-century religion, and it is now clear that the post-Puritan churches were losing ground to Baptists, Methodists, Disciples of Christ, and a host of sectarian and immigrant churches. Methodists, Baptists, and immigrant Catholics became numerically dominant, and their social and political behavior was very different from that of Rochester's Yankee Presbyterians.

I applaud the democratizing and de-centering thrust of the recent literature, and I agree that my sources and my discussion of them were keyed on one tradition and not on the whole of American religion. But I must point out that the reformist revivalism described in *A Shopkeeper's Millennium* became the center of a national religious and political discourse: it was the Finneyite middle class that was the popular base of the northern Whig Party, the moralistic bogeyman of the Democrats (hundreds of thousands of Methodists and Baptists among them), and what Southerners were thinking about when they railed against meddlesome, self-righteous "Yankees." Borrowing an essential distinction from Max Weber, let me put it this way: the evangelicalism of Charles Grandison Finney was not the dominant religion of the northern United States; it was the religion—this is a central point of the book—of Northerner who were becoming dominant.

Finally, my crimes against women. *A Shopkeeper's Millennium* attempts to throw light on the process whereby Northern politics came, quite abruptly in the 1830s, to be organized by religion. I argued that changes in relations between work and domestic life were at the heart of religious change in Rochester; then I followed evangelical men out into male politics and male public life. New studies in women's history quickly called my strategy into question: they stayed indoors and reconstructed the mother-centered middle-class family, pointing out that women far outnumbered men in evangelical churches, and disclosing the domestic character of the message preached in those churches. These studies argued forcefully that middle-class evangelicalism (and middle-class culture generally) was about gender, not class. They argued just as forcefully that most of the cultural work that made the middle class was performed by women. I nodded to all that, but not with the emphasis that could have warded off justifiable criticisms of my male-centered study. Yet I continue to argue (as I argued in 1978) that the privatization and feminization of middle-class domestic life is unthinkable without reference to larger transformations in society, that the middle-class family and its culture were deeply implicated in those transformations and in the ways in which they worked out in history.

It should be clear by now that were I writing *A Shopkeeper's Millennium* today, I would do it differently. I would still base the study in the recoverable facts about church members. (It is good to know who one is talking about: in this case, it was the new entrepreneurial families that rose up within the market revolution.) I would continue to look at work relationships, family forms (but with much greater attention to women), and residential patterns. But I would make only the most modest effort to explain religious conversion in terms of such factors. Instead, I would discuss revival conversion as a key event (for most actors, the event that shaped all the others) in the making of the private, self-governing individual. I would also continue to argue that the whole process had something to do with the rise of democratic capitalism, and I would not change the title. It still describes what happened in Rochester.

Soon after publishing this book, I was at an academic conference in Italy. The revered labor historian Herbert Gutman and I walked out of a restaurant and, in perfect tough-guy Brooklynese, he said to me: "That book you wrote. It's fucked-up. [pause] But it's right." As in many other things, I continue to think that Herb Gutman was a wise and good man.

A SHOPKEEPER'S MILLENNIUM

Introduction

IN November 1830 the evangelist Charles Grandison Finney faced an audience of merchants, master craftsmen, and their families at Third Presbyterian Church in Rochester, New York. The people at Third Church were inheritors of New England Calvinism, and they knew that the world was beyond their control. In 1815 the town's Presbyterians had declared themselves impotent before a God who "foreordained whatsoever comes to pass." Ten years later the founders of Second Church reaffirmed the belief that men could alter neither their individual spiritual states nor the shape of their society. Revivals had been eroding these beliefs since the 1790s, and there were people at Third Church who had rejected them altogether. But most Rochester Protestants still inhabited a world where events, in H. Richard Niebuhr's phrase, were a glove on the hand of God.[1]

Finney had been fighting that idea since the middle 1820s, in revivals that had taken him throughout northern and central New York and, most recently, into Philadelphia and New York City. Now he turned to the audience at Third Church and completed the revolution. "God has made man a moral free agent," he declared Evil was the product not of innate depravity but of choices made by selfish men and women. Sin and disorder would disappear when they chose good over evil and convinced others to do the same. Finney stared down from the pulpit and said flatly that if Christians united and dedicated their lives to the task, they could convert the world and

bring on the millennium in three months.[2] The evangelist
finished, and his audience stirred. Then scores of people rose
from their seats, many of them weeping, and pledged their
lives to Jesus. With that act they left the imperfect and confin-
ing world that God had made for corrupt man, and entered a
world where men worked ceaselessly to make themselves and
others perfect.

Similar scenes took place in towns and cities throughout the
northern United States in the winter of 1830–31. The revival
made new hearts in hundreds of thousands of middle-class
men and women, and set them off on a massive and remarkably successful crusade to remake society in God's name. This
book attempts to explain why it happened.

1

The awakening of 1831 climaxed a generation of revivals
that historians have called the Second Great Awakening. But
while it was continuous with earlier enthusiasms, it had a
unity, an intentionality, and a sheer size that set it apart. The
awakening began near the turn of the century in the villages
of New England and in isolated Yankee colonies in western
New York. Within that region enthusiasm sputtered for
twenty years, arbitrarily descending on one congregation or
community while neighboring churches slept. The gradual,
provincial character of the revival was disturbed by ripples of
enthusiasm in 1821 and again in 1826. Then it shattered in the
national revival of 1831, and in a flurry of excitement that
lasted until the economic collapse of 1837. Church membership relative to the population doubled between 1800 and 1835,
and most of the growth came after 1830. The churches of New
England grew by one-third in 1831. In Rochester, church
membership doubled in six months, and there were similar
gains in communities throughout the northern United States.
Lyman Beecher, who rivals Finney as the era's most promi-

nent evangelist, declared that the awakening of 1831 "was the greatest work of God, and the greatest revival of religion, that the world has ever seen."[3]

Beecher based his statement not only on the number of conversions but on a profound change in what conversion meant. For the revival of 1831, more than any other event, marked the acceptance of an activist and millennialist evangelicalism as the faith of the northern middle class. New England revivals in the first quarter of the century had been quiet, decorous affairs, presided over by settled ministers who wanted only to reinstate conformity to God's laws among God's people. (In a world where God alone determined who was saved, mass evangelism was useless and vaguely blasphemous.) Lyman Beecher, when he heard that Charles Finney and other New Yorkers had devised ways of "getting up" revivals, promised to call out the militia if they brought their heresy into New England. But in 1831, with the revival exploding all around him, he invited Finney into his own Boston church.[4] Within a few years free agency, perfectionism, and millennialism were middle-class orthodoxy.

They were powerful ideas, and in the 1830s they underlay a missionary crusade that transformed society and politics in the United States. It was Gilbert Barnes, a historian of the antislavery movement writing in the 1930s, who "discovered" the revival of 1831. Barnes wanted to explain why, in the 1830s, critics of slavery rejected gradualist techniques, recruited thousands of new supporters, and attacked the South's peculiar institution as a national evil that demanded immediate abolition. He analyzed the rhetoric and tactics of the movement and the sources of its support, and argued convincingly that antislavery immediatism was a direct outgrowth of the revival of 1830–31.[5]

Since then, Barnes's discovery has been extended to the whole array of antebellum reform. The temperance, moral reform, and missionary societies of the 1820s had been organizations of gentlemen who wished to slow the course of social and political change and reinforce their domination over a hopelessly godless multitude. In the early 1830s newly converted evangelicals invaded all of these organizations and took most of them over. The new reformers did not want to control the inevitable excesses of drunkards and prostitutes and Jacksonian Democrats. They wanted to liberate them from their sins. Through individual conversion and public example, and increasingly through mass politics and outright coercion, they promised to eliminate sin from society and pave the way for the Second Coming. The same millennial hopes guided a dramatic increase in home missions, and they shaped the beginnings of organized anti-Catholicism in this country.[6]

The reform societies are parts of an accessible and public history, and we have known about religious influences within them for a long time. More recently, scholars have begun the systematic study of everyday social life, and again they are confronting the evangelicals and their works. The 1820s witnessed the beginnings of large-scale manufacturing in American cities, and with it came attempts to subject farm boys and preindustrial artisans to the discipline and monotony of modern work. Historians of labor are finding that in the 1830s proto-industrialists fought that battle with religious weapons. Their most favored means of combating drunkenness, spontaneous holidays, and inattention to work were the temperance society, the Sunday school, and the revival. Indeed many masters and manufacturers saw industrialization as a civilizing mission: they believed in their hearts that in proletarianizing workmen they were rescuing them from barbarism and granting them the benefits of Christian discipline. The workingmen, of course, saw things differently, and the crucial first generation of industrial conflict in this country was fought largely along religious lines.[7]

The revival was bound up with equally profound changes in middle-class family life. New England Protestants had always seen households as models for society at large. In the seventeenth and eighteenth centuries, families were expected to govern the excesses of their members, and the father wielded absolute authority in God's name. Evangelicals continued to view households as social models, but in their scheme women, servants, and even the smallest children were capable of choosing between good and evil. The idea of moral free agency demanded that householders cultivate the uniqueness and autonomy of the persons under their care. That task fell more and more to mothers. They were warned not to beat their children or frighten them with stories about innate depravity, but to mix discipline with love, and to develop moral sensibilities that would make them useful citizens of a Christian republic. Books dispensing such advice began appearing near 1830. Most of them were written by evangelical clergymen.[8]

By the middle 1830s the revival had entered national politics. Students of voting behavior and party formation in New York and Michigan have discovered a confused and fragmented opposition to Jacksonian Democrats coalescing in the 1830s, with support centered in areas hit hardest by the revival, and with issues and organizational techniques taken directly from the evangelists. When elections had pitted Federalists against Jeffersonian Republicans, members of different denominations had lined up on opposing sides. Now political contests found evangelical Protestants on one side and nearly everyone else on the other. Subsequent studies have traced that division into the twentieth century.[9] The voting studies describe a correlation between religion and politics: from the 1830s on, party preference traces to religious belief. But with that established, they declare politics a reflex of inherited culture. In doing so, they ignore the historical process in which the correlation was made. It certainly did not exist before 1830. The unity and militance of Whig-evangelical voters may have stemmed less from cultural inheritance than from recent events, events that were bound up intimately with the great revival.

Whig politicians, industrial moralizers, temperance advocates, missionaries, and family reformers worked tirelessly to build a world that replaced force, barbarism, and unrestrained passion with Christian self-control. That was not the idea of a few visionaries and cranks and political opportunists. It was the moral imperative around which the northern middle class became a class. In 1825 a northern businessman dominated his wife and children, worked irregular hours, consumed enormous amounts of alcohol, and seldom voted or went to church. Ten years later the same man went to church twice a week, treated his family with gentleness and love, drank nothing but water, worked steady hours and forced his employees to do the same, campaigned for the Whig Party, and spent his spare time convincing others that if they organized their lives in similar ways, the world would be perfect. To put it simply, the middle class became resolutely bourgeois between 1825 and 1835. And at every step, that transformation bore the stamp of evangelical Protestantism.

Scholars noting all of this have argued that businessmen were adapting to an expanding market economy, that they were devising new ways of dominating others, or simply that they were becoming modern. They were indeed doing those things. But they did them in religious ways. An explanation of how the middle class became modern (or bourgeois, or democratic) must come to terms with revival religion.

2

If so much came out of the revival of 1830–31, precisely what went into it? The rich literature on American revivals contains surprisingly few causal statements. Scholars assume that revivals were responses to widespread spiritual unrest, but few have attempted to describe its specific content. Evangelical America was, after all, the America of Andrew Jackson and Alexis de Tocqueville. The people who flocked to Charles Finney's meetings had experienced an abrupt and decisive commercial revolution in agriculture, rapid territorial expansion, the beginnings of industrialization and sustained urban growth, the democratization of politics—a generation of change that transformed Jefferson's republic of self-governing communities into Jackson's boisterous capitalist democracy.

America in 1830, we are told, was a society in which normative and institutional restraints of every kind had fallen apart. Rather than pick through the rubble of discarded social controls, historians of religion generalize that revivals represented a quest for community or emotional stability among a nation of rootless individualists. Those who single out causes sometimes point to the insecurities of the new rich, but just as often to the attempts of bypassed elites to reestablish their dominance. Others look to the disruption of kin networks and neighborly controls which attended the migration of thousands of families west and into the cities. Still others point to the peculiar problems of adolescence in an open society. But most follow Tocqueville and gesture vaguely at the collapse of authority at every level. Established churches, stable neighborhoods, families, authoritative local elites: these and internalized restraints of every kind were swept away by the market, by migration and personal ambition, and by the universal acceptance of democratic ideas. Revivals were a means of building order and a sense of common purpose among sovereign, footloose, and money-hungry individualists.[10]

These historians have been interested in religion, not in its foundations in the social order. Their causal statements are vague, principally because they are consumers rather than producers of social history, and social historians have given them little with which to work. We have more generalizations and less solid information on society in the years 1815 to 1850 than on any other period in the American past.[11] We know, for instance, that the extension of the market after 1815 revolutionized the ways in which people lived. But what precisely were the effects on ordinary persons, and which of those effects translated into religious tension? We know that Americans are a mobile people and that movement from place to place seems to have accelerated after 1800. But what, really, did migration do to the texture of everyday life, and were the most mobile really more prone to revivalism than others? We know that Jacksonian America was full of men on the make. How many made it? And was it the new rich who swarmed into the churches? We have been told over and over that the early nineteenth century was an age of institutional breakdown. Which institutions broke down? Which persisted? Every student of revivals assumes that they were a response to disorder in the lives of ordinary men and women. But we do not know precisely who joined churches during revivals. Until we do, speculation on the sources of their religious unrest seems a little out of place. Terms such as "culture strain" and "social atomization" are not enough. Most Americans were somehow strained in the 1820s and 1830s. But which ones found comfort in revivals, and why?

Answers to that question will remain vague and unsatisfying until we know more about the people who converted during revivals. Beyond that, we need some conception of the social processes that are tied most sensitively to religious belief, and whose derangement would be likely to elicit a religious response.

The sociological explanation of religion that has guided this study stems from the work of Emile Durkheim.[12] Durkheim and his followers assume (and here they agree with the historians of revivals) a close relationship between religious belief and those social activities that are surrounded by conscience, moral authority, and internalized restraint. Moral rules are of course created socially, and they continue to be grounded in specific social processes. But once created they take on autonomous power, governing and legitimating the relationships that made them. They become what Durkheim called social facts: habits and ways of feeling that shape individual consciousness and behavior, yet exist outside the individual and coerce him independent of his will.[13]

This narrows the search for the origins of revivals, for not every social encounter generates social facts. Those that do tend to be stable, reciprocal, and nearly universal within a given society. Most of all, they are relationships that are necessary to the smooth and continuous functioning of the community. Marriage, for example, is a social fact.[14] In most societies a certain amount of bickering between husbands and wives is taken for granted. But if a man stops fighting his wife and begins fighting his marriage, and if that event is repeated in society until "marriage" itself is called into question, that is a religious problem. A marriage is objectively nothing more than two people in a social relationship. But as every married person knows, it is something more than that. And that something seems peculiarly sensitive to religion.

Why do some social relationships become invested with moral authority while others do not? Let us stay with the example of marriage. First, it is a stable, universal relationship that remains the same through space and time. Marriages come and go, but "marriage" spans the generations. It is independent of individual husbands and wives, yet it controls each of them in powerful ways. Second, it is socially necessary. Each marriage institutes a family with jurisdiction over crucial spheres of life: giving food and shelter to its members, raising children, providing legitimate means of sexual release, and so on. In the course of satisfying these needs each marriage develops a pattern of cooperation that is both unique and culturally prescribed. This pattern is internalized by both spouses, and it shapes their identities both as individuals and as participants in a culture. Thus marriage performs the twin function of sustaining individual identity and making society

possible—and it does both in ways that are invisible and com-
pelling. That is why marriage is charged with religious meaning, and why deviations from it are punished not merely as
breaches of cultural norms but as sacrilege.

Not only marriage but other key relationships assume this
corporate, otherworldly character. Extended kinship networks, particularly if they control such functions as the choice
of marriage partners or the allocation of group resources, com-
prise such a set of relationships. Sometimes work groups are
surrounded by religious controls, sometimes the local community as a whole. Almost invariably, the social relations that
surround the making of group decisions—from family con-
claves to town meetings to national legislatures—are governed
by such constraints. A breakdown in any of these relationships
creates, for the persons involved and for the society of which
they are members, a religious problem. And if the breakdown
is widespread—if not only individual marriages but "marriage" itself is falling apart—it must be resolved at a general
level. Among Protestant Christians, solutions to such massive
spiritual crises take the form of what we call revivals.

Thus the Durkheimians provide a means of explaining
revivals without resorting to easy generalizations on the character of the national social order. For if religion is grounded
in specific kinds of social relationships, then rapid religious
change points to dislocations not in society generally but in
those relationships. Most historical accounts translate readily
into this vocabulary, for they place revivals within a society in
which free individuals related to each other only on an *ad hoc*,
voluntary basis. That, of course, would constitute a religious
problem of enormous dimensions. But it is possible that in
some areas of life old modes of cooperation survived the social
and economic transformation of the early nineteenth century,
and can thus be discounted as precipitants of revivals. The
method outlined here demands that we identify persons who
participated in revivals, then locate social relationships in

which those individuals had experienced the collapse of old reciprocal norms.

Happily, there are ways of doing that. In recent years historians have devised quantitative means of analyzing family structure, kinship relations, political conflict, occupational and geographic mobility, patterns of association, and a variety of other phenomena that had been beyond the range of systematic study. The result has been a series of studies of the family, of political behavior, of occupational success and failure, and so on. Seldom, however, have these techniques been used to explain cultural change or the rise and fall of social movements. Yet the potential is there.[15] With these methods we can demonstrate ways in which various changes intersected in the lives of persons who joined churches during revivals, and thus define the specific social strains that underlay the rise of evangelicalism. We can, in short, systematically trace the social origins of revival religion.

The approach is best tested in a single community. As the site of that investigation I have chosen Rochester, New York. Generally the makers of case studies claim that the subject of their work is somehow representative of communities that experienced whatever phenomena they are trying to explain. That is not the case with Rochester. The sequence of rapid urbanization, religious revival, and political and social reorganization struck that community with uncommon force. Rochester was the first of the inland cities created after 1815 by the commercialization of agriculture. In 1812 the site of Rochester was unbroken wilderness. By 1830 the forest had given way to a city of 10,000, the marketing and manufacturing center for a broad and prosperous agricultural hinterland. Rochester was the capital of western New York's revival-seared "Burned-over District," and a clearinghouse for religious enthusiasms throughout the 1820s and 1830s. The city holds a special place in the history of revivals, for Charles Finney's triumph there in 1830–31 was the most spectacular event within the national revival of that year. In short, Rochester was the most thoroughly evangelized of American cities.[16]

Were revivals a response to insecurities engendered by a normless, dog-eat-dog economy? Did they result from spiritual emptiness among men and women who moved too often to establish new social ties or maintain old ones? America's first inland boom town seems a good place to test those propositions. What accounts for the increasingly urban, middle-class character of revivals after 1830? Rochester was the nation's newest city in that year, and Finney's revival there more than any other single event marked the movement of enthusiasm into the cities. What precisely were the links between revivals and the transformation of politics and reform in the 1830s? Again, Rochester was a center of those developments.

The pages that follow attempt a systematic explanation of Charles Finney's revival in Rochester. The attempt is not based upon tourists' tales, theological disputes, or the reminiscences of ministers, although it makes use of all of them. The focus is upon the biographies of the converts themselves, reconstructed from church records, newspapers, genealogical materials, tax lists, city directories, census schedules, petitions sent from Rochester to various agencies of government, and a surprising number of diaries and letters left by participants in the revival. These materials are used to place Finney's converts within four crucial spheres of social experience: domestic life, work, community relations, and politics. The first chapter determines the effects of migration and participation in the boom-town economy upon entrepreneurs and their families. Chapter II describes the transformation of work and community relationships in the 1820s. Chapters III and IV analyze the institutional and ideological framework of politics in the 1820s, and survey the temperance, Sabbatarian, and Antimasonic crusades of those years. The fifth chapter describes the revival itself. The sixth describes its aftermath.

1
Economy

CHARLES FINNEY came to Rochester via the Erie Canal in the autumn of 1830. The route from Albany took him through the Mohawk Valley, then onto the broad plain that forms the southern shore of Lake Ontario. The last fifty miles passed through recently settled land, and on both sides of the canal Finney saw farmhouses and bustling villages surrounded by endless yellow wheatfields. East of the Genesee River, the fields stopped abruptly and Rochester began. Finney's boat crossed a line of new stores and houses, passed high over the river on a stone aqueduct, and delivered him to the center of the nation's newest city.

It was a city with the look and feel of a country town.[1] Near the boat landing Finney picked his way through horses and wagons that visiting farmers had left at the central intersection. Glancing east, he saw and heard country people hawking produce from stalls on the bridge over the Genesee, while underneath them the famed Rochester mills ground mountains of local wheat into flour. A half block west, farmers auctioned wagons and livestock from the steps of a pretentious new courthouse. Across from the courthouse, sidewalks were clogged with farm families and with displays of shoes and clothing, nails, butter churns, farm tools, hats, and other simple manufactured goods. Had Finney looked upstairs or into the back rooms of some of the stores, he would have found that most Rochesterians were engaged in making those goods. The streets were filled not only with farmers and merchants but with what Finney may have felt was an uncomfortable number of urban workingmen.

Turning south on Fitzhugh Street, the evangelist passed between stately Episcopal and Presbyterian churches and left the downtown crowds behind. Before him stretched a quiet, tree-lined block of Greek Revival mansions. At the end of the block he found the door of a merchant and land speculator named Josiah Bissell. Bissell had invited the preacher to Rochester, and it was his neighbors who would attend Finney's meetings. They were the kinds of provincial entrepreneurs with whom Finney did his best work, men like those who governed the Connecticut and New York villages in which he had grown up. For the wealthiest men in Rochester were merchants, millers, and manufacturers engaged directly in an agricultural economy.

TOWN AND COUNTRY

Cities like Rochester were new in the 1820s. A generation earlier, every urban place in America had been a seaport, standing with its back to the countryside. Merchants in Boston and New York had more contact with their counterparts in London and the West Indies than with farmers a few miles away. Town and country were separate worlds. But after 1815 improvements in inland transportation extended the market and turned farmers into businessmen; inland cities shot up overnight to process and ship farm products, and sometimes to turn them into finished goods for sale back to the farmers. It was in the 1820s that cities and large towns began continuously to grow faster than the countryside. And it was in that decade that Rochester became the fastest-growing community in the United States.[2] Standing at the junction of the Erie Canal and the Genesee River, Rochester was the most spectacular of the new cities created by the commercialization of agriculture.

The Genesee country was among the prizes of the American Revolution. Title fell to the state of Massachusetts, then to successive groups of speculators, and finally to farmers.[3] In the 1790s New Englanders crossed the mountains and began colonizing the Great Lakes Plain; the Genesee Valley was among their first stops. Early in the new century the wilderness gave way to tilled fields and pastures and neat Yankee villages. Links with the east were primitive, and the first settlers produced little more than what they and their neighbors used. The principal crop was Indian corn, and farmers and their animals ate that themselves. There was, of course, a small surplus. A trickle of livestock and logs made its way down the Susquehanna River and into Pennsylvania. Even smaller amounts made the tortuous and expensive trip overland to Albany.[4] But most went downriver to Rochester.

For many years the nearness of an unfriendly Canadian border and the fevers that threatened settlers near the lake kept farmers out of the lower Genesee. But the perfect mill site at the falls (the river drops two hundred feet within what is now downtown Rochester) had attracted attention from the beginning. In 1812 optimistic promoters laid out the village of Rochesterville. The town milled Genesee produce and sent it over the lake and up the St. Lawrence to Montreal, a touchy and unpredictable market subject to regulation by a foreign government that had farmers of its own.[5] At the same time, primitive transportation kept the Genesee country largely dependent on its own resources. Scores of merchants and artisans set up shop in Rochester to sell goods imported from outside the region, and to turn livestock into salt meat and shoes and harnesses, wheat into flour and whiskey, and logs into lumber and furniture—all for sale back to the countryside. When workmen digging the Erie Canal reached Rochester in 1821, they found a busy village of 1,500 growing in symbiosis with the farming community of the Genesee Valley.

Canal workers finished the through route to New York City

in 1823. Overnight, the Genesee Valley became one of the great grain-growing regions of the world, and Rochester was America's first inland boom town. Assured cheap and easy access to the New York market, settlers plowed pastures and cornfields and planted wheat up to their doorways. Tilled acreage south of Rochester doubled between 1822 and 1835. Closer to the canal and to the mills at Rochester, it tripled. The region's only city stood at the center of its richest agricultural county.[6] Rochester processed Genesee wheat and sent it on to New York City, and the growth of both town and country was measurable in barrels of flour. The town exported 26,000 barrels in 1818, a good pre-canal year. Ten years later the figure stood at 200,000, and by the close of the 1830s Rochester produced a half-million barrels of flour annually.[7] In the same years the village grew from a few hundred to 20,000 persons.

Rochester was first and last a mill town. Four- and five-story stone flour mills lined the river at the city's center and dominated the skyline as well as the economy. Of the town's 117 manufacturing establishments in 1827, 10 were flour mills. These accounted for 55 percent of Rochester's investment in manufactures, and a full 71 percent of its manufacturing output.[8] Built on plans developed in the 1790s by Oliver Evans, the mills were lessons in what could be done with water power and money. Boats pulled up alongside them and workmen shoveled grain into buckets on a vertical conveyor. Wheat went up the side, onto the top floors, and through machinery that cleaned it and ground it into flour, spread it on the floor to cool, picked it up, and dropped it into barrels. A visitor left one of these establishments gasping that it was "as full of machinery as the case of a watch."[9]

The mills hired few men directly, and they made great fortunes for even fewer. But they were the linchpin in the Rochester economy. Commercialization enabled farmers to trade their surplus for manufactured goods, and the mills drew them into Rochester, paid them cash for their wheat, and sent them onto the streets looking for things to buy. Much of what they bought was imported. Westbound traffic on the canal carried finished goods as well as emigrants, and Rochester merchants stocked their shelves with finished goods from New York City and around the world. Its position at midpoint on the canal also made Rochester the wholesaler to country merchants, adding another strand to the ties that bound town and country.

But imported goods were expensive. For everyday necessities the farmers continued to rely upon craftsmen in Rochester, and their insatiable demand turned the village into a manufacturing city. More than half the adult men in Rochester were skilled artisans, most of them engaged in turning local raw materials into finished goods for sale back to the countryside. The sixty-five workshops of 1823 concentrated on the necessities and little luxuries of rural life: guns and nails, shoes, hats, woolen cloth, wagons, furniture, farm tools—even jewelry and mirrors.[10] These last testify to a growing prosperity and urbanity in the countryside. By the late 1820s merchants' stocks of imported silks and fine wines had grown, and the Rochester market supported three bookstores. Artisans now made carriages as well as wagons, and builders moved out to duplicate Rochester's Greek Revival mansions on the greens of Palmyra and Geneseo and other valley towns. In 1835 a Rochester manufactory began filling the parlors of those homes with that seldom-played symbol of the Anglo-American bourgeoisie, the piano—testimony to the "increasing wealth and improving taste of the people of the surrounding country, as well as of the city."[11]

Most Rochester entrepreneurs made their money in direct dealings with farmers, and engagement in a rural economy and conformity to its norms sustained a peculiarly countrified urban business community. Of the ninety-two merchants, millers, and manufacturers who made up Rochester's richest tenth of taxpayers in 1827, thirty-two can be traced to their places of birth. A full 84 percent of these were natives of inland New England and thus shared the cultural inheritance of their customers in the hinterland. They shared more than that, for most had moved into western New York early in their lives and had done business in the villages surrounding Rochester. Of the twenty-nine whose residences prior to arriving in Rochester are known, 59 percent came from towns that were within fifty miles of the city. Many of them kept substantial investments in the villages. Others relied on rural relatives and friends for capital and business information. And they retained mentalities that, along with their money and their strategic locations, made them legitimate spokesmen for the more prosperous elements of Genesee Valley society. City ministers frequently exchanged pulpits with their colleagues in the hinterland. Rural-based agricultural societies and committees for the distribution of Bibles and temperance tracts welcomed the participation of Rochester entrepreneurs and often accepted their leadership, and it was no accident that four of the five state committeemen of the overwhelmingly rural Antimasonic Party were Rochester businessmen.[12] For while Rochester grew into a city, it kept the economic functions and the business elite of a country market town.

Of course, not every store and workshop catered to the country trade. For a time in the 1820s the canal made Rochester the chief provisions market for migrants on their way farther west, and canal travelers continued to spend money in Rochester even after such newer towns as Buffalo, Cleveland, and Detroit had taken up the bulk of their trade. In addition, the Rochester working class was large enough to support scores of groceries and small retail stores. It was here—and apparently only here—that men who had little in common with the farmers could prosper. Every known Irish Catholic businessman, for instance, avoided the country trade. Their leader, Henry O'Reilley, owned a Democratic newspaper which, if voting returns are any indication, found few readers in the countryside. Peter Lynch operated a combined grocery and boardinghouse on one of Rochester's poorest streets. And his countrymen James Buchan and Patrick Kearney, the richest Irishmen in town, provided workingmen and "gentlemen traveling" with cheap ready-made clothing.[13] Men who entered the country trade without meeting its cultural and behavioral standards learned painful lessons. When marginal retailers failed during the panic of 1837, one of the more substantial merchants listed the reasons why. The Scotch Dry Goods Store was run by foreigners who published misleading advertising and hired dishonest and impudent clerks. Hamilton Leonard kept bad company and spent too much time at the theater. And E. W. Collins, who cheated his customers repeatedly, "ought to be among savages and not among the citizens of Rochester."[14]

A few of these outsiders operated substantial businesses, but none made great fortunes. For Rochester's real money was in the country trade. The nature of that trade and of the men recruited into it produced urban entrepreneurs who retained the social practices and the moral vision of village storekeepers.

FAMILY CAPITALISM

The merchants, millers, and master craftsmen who flocked to Charles Finney's meetings worked successfully within the limits imposed by the Rochester market. The first of those limits was set by the farmers. The people of the Genesee country were natives of inland New England: clannish, self-righteous, and suspicious of outsiders.[15] Wealth in Rochester went only to men who could win and hold their goodwill. The second limit derived from economic scale: the more lucrative operations demanded more capital than aspiring businessmen had at hand. Rochester entrepreneurs shared the risks and rewards of enterprise with others—usually relatives and long-term associates. Individual fortunes were meshed with social networks that linked wealthy families with each other and with similar families in the hinterland, and entrepreneurial behavior was typified by caution and cooperation, and not by ungoverned individual ambition. The result was a remarkably orderly and closed community of entrepreneurs.

We begin with land speculators. Rochester grew from a wilderness to a city overnight, and the first fortunes went to men who bought and sold the wilderness. As settlement accelerated in 1815, central Rochester was held in four parcels: the Hundred-Acre Tract and the Frankfort Tract west of the river, and the Andrews-Atwater Tract and Enos Stone's farm on the east side. The Hundred-Acre Tract was bought in 1803 by three gentlemen from Maryland: Charles Carroll, William Fitzhugh, and Nathaniel Rochester. The Fitzhughs moved north and established themselves as one of the leading families on the upper Genesee. They kept their large holdings in Rochester and (in partnership with Nathaniel Rochester's son-in-law Jonothan Child) invested in boom-town construction projects. The Episcopal parish register records a few of their marriages and births in the 1820s. But William Fitzhugh and his family stayed up the valley, leaving the administration of their Rochester holdings to partners and to his son-in-law Frederick Backus, a Rochester physician. The Carrolls joined them on the upper Genesee, and sent one son downriver to manage their investments.[16]

But it was Nathaniel Rochester who moved into the Genesee first, and who gave his name to the village at the falls.[17] At the head of his family, a caravan of wagons and carriages, and an indeterminate number of slaves, he rode up the Susquehanna and into the Genesee country in 1810. He settled at Dansville, where he operated a 400-acre farm and looked after investments scattered all over the region. Prospects for settlement at the falls brightened with the end of war in 1815, and Rochester sold his farm and bought another in Bloomfield.

From there he made frequent seventeen-mile visits to his holdings at the falls. In 1818 he moved to Rochester. With the center of activities now at Rochester, members of his extensive family began filtering into town. The colonel's son-in-law Jonothan Child followed him in from Bloomfield. From Bath came his son William, already one of the leading Bucktail Republican politicians in the state. The connection grew with the arrival of Rochester's son Thomas and his son-in-law Harvey Montgomery, who had been in the dry-goods business in nearby Parma, and another son-in-law, Dr. Anson Colman. Along with their friends, associates, and distant kin, the Rochesters formed a powerful clan whose size defies full description. Every Fourth of July the colonel gave a picnic on the grounds of his house on Spring Street. It was the most elaborate and reputedly the largest of the town's social gatherings in the early 1820s. Only members and close friends of the family were invited.[18]

North of Colonel Rochester's holdings stood the Frankfort Tract, bought in 1810 by Matthew, Francis, and David Brown in partnership with Thomas Mumford and John McKay.[19] A Massachusetts family, the Browns had been among the founders of Rome, New York, in 1794. Early in the new century, Francis Brown went to live with an uncle who traded with the Indians in Detroit. It was on one of his visits home that he looked into prospects on the lower Genesee and recommended them to the family. They bought land along the west bank in 1810. Francis and Matthew Brown left the family seat in Rome and moved onto the new holdings. Their cousin Warren followed, speculating in mercantile ventures in Rochester and the surrounding towns before settling at Penfield, just outside Rochester. Francis Brown soon married a daughter of the proprietor of that town, and the family edged steadily out into the countryside. Their partner, Thomas Mumford, a Yale-educated lawyer who had settled east of Rochester at Cayuga Bridge, bought out John McKay, and went into partnership with his son William and his brother Silas. Thomas and Silas Mumford stayed at Cayuga Bridge. Young William came to Rochester and managed the family holdings.

The pattern of family partnerships and family ties extending into the hinterland held up east of the river, where Samuel J. Andrews and Caleb Atwater bought a string of mill sites and the land behind them in 1812.[20] Atwater was a physician, merchant, and realtor who had been among the first settlers at Canandaigua, the pre-canal commercial center of the Genesee Valley. Andrews was Atwater's brother-in-law and a merchant near New Haven, Connecticut. Along with the Whittleseys of New Haven, they bought Rochester land. Andrews settled in Rochester in 1815 and built the town's first stone building at what became the corner of St. Paul and Main. His son Samuel G. Andrews, along with William and Frederick Whittlesey, came in from New Haven and took over active promotion of the Andrews-Atwater Tract.

The last large parcel was Enos Stone's farm.[21] Like several families who became their Rochester neighbors, the Stones were old residents of Lenox, Massachusetts. With some of those neighbors, Enos Sr. bought Brighton Township (east Rochester) in 1789. His son Orange settled there the following year. His younger sons Alvah and Enos Jr. stayed in Lenox until 1810, when he gave them each a large farm on the Genesee. The father remained in Lenox until his wife died in 1816. Then he moved and lived out the rest of his life as a member of Enos Jr.'s household at the falls. Alvah and Orange remained gentlemen farmers in the nearby townships of Brighton and Penfield. But Enos Jr.'s land lay directly in the path of the Genesee boom town. He held on shrewdly, selling a piece in 1817 but keeping most of the farm intact until prices reached a peak in 1826. Then he sold it and became very rich.

These were the men who owned Rochester before it was built. Certainly they were a diverse group, ranging from New England hill farmers to seaport merchants to members of the

Maryland gentry. But they had much in common. All of them came to Rochester as members of business networks made up largely or entirely of their relatives. Enos Stone, with his father in the house and two brothers in adjoining townships, headed the simplest of these families. Nathaniel Rochester headed the most complex: a fantastic labyrinth of connected sons and sons-in-law (not to mention two more sons managing family land in Missouri and Kentucky), old neighbors and business associates from Maryland and from up the valley, and an indeterminate but large number of distant kin in Rochester. Each of these combinations included prominent citizens of other western New York towns: the Mumfords at Cayuga Bridge, the Stone brothers in Brighton and Penfield, Moses Atwater in Canandaigua, the Carrolls and Fitzhughs in Livingston County. From the beginning, large business operations in Rochester hinged on cooperation within and between the wealthier families of the Genesee Valley.

The landowners of 1815 were firstcomers. While they owned a wilderness and made money selling it to newcomers, they may have sensed that the transformation of family land into urban real estate would spell the end of them and their kind. That, however, was not the case. The country trade remained the source of great fortunes throughout the 1820s and 1830s, and we have seen already that ties between the countryside and the entrepreneurial elite remained strong even at the height of the boom.[22] And within Rochester, the rich men of 1827 continued to organize their operations along family lines. Few of these men had enough money to build flour mills or speculate in land for themselves, and they joined forces with members of their families. The result of participation in the boom-town business world was not a collapse of kinship but the strengthening of old family loyalties and the invention of new ones.

The nature and extent of those relationships can be demonstrated by comparison with an older and more established

elite: the overseas merchants of Salem in 1810. In Salem, where
the marriage of family and enterprise is almost legendary, 42
percent of the merchants were in business with relatives.[23]
Among the richest tenth of Rochester property holders in
1827, the figure was an identical 42 percent. That, of course,
is startling evidence of a strong relationship between kinship
and enterprise in Rochester, and we might be tempted to leave
it at that. But the relationships underneath those uniform
totals are equally revealing. The formation of Salem partnerships was governed by what must be called dynastic considera-
tions.[24] Agreements between brothers were most common,
but they were nearly equaled by combinations of fathers and
sons. These arrangements united family assets in a single male
line. Uncle-nephew partnerships served the same purpose, for
many of them joined childless men with their brothers' sons.
Such agreements reunited fortunes that had been split by inheritance, sending the fragments to a single male heir.[25] The
Salem arrangements speak of a strong corporate sense of family: fully 48 percent of family partnerships crossed genera-
tional lines.

In Rochester that figure dropped to 33 percent, while there
was a sharp increase in the number of agreements between
brothers-in-law. In part this was due to the relative absence of
fathers and uncles in Rochester's young elite. Businessmen
and manufacturers had left older relatives at home, and most
were too young to have adult sons.[26] But even more, the
Rochester pattern reflected the need to increase blocks of capital rather than preserve them. The young Salemite who went
into business with his father or paternal uncle kept family
resources intact and provided them with an heir. But he seldom brought new money into the concern. In alliances with
in-laws, the Rochesterians merged the fortunes of separate
families and thus increased the potential pool of resources.
Perhaps the Rochester pattern reflects a weakening of ties
between generations. (In the rural New England homeland,

such ties had been eroding for a hundred years.[27]) But it points more strongly to the invention of new loyalties between distant kin and to a broadening concept of family.

Alliances between in-laws increased available capital and at the same time entrusted its use to men who shared familial as well as contractual obligations. Even businessmen who formed partnerships with non-relatives did not join with strangers but sought out men whose long-term friendship and association established them as surrogate kin. When Josiah Bissell joined with Harvey and Elisha Ely, he was continuing a partnership that had existed at home in Pittsfield, Massachusetts. The merchants Charles Hill and A. V. T. Leavitt had grown up together in Bethlehem, Connecticut. And young Everard Peck entered the publishing business with Silas Andrews, under whom he had served an apprenticeship in Hartford.[28] The result of all this might be termed a fraternalization of economic relationships—both within wealthy families and between them. Such arrangements united large segments of the business elite. Altogether, 55 percent of these men formed partnerships with others who ranked among the richest 10 percent of property holders. Twenty-seven percent formed more than one of these alliances; 12 percent formed three or more. Rochester's entrepreneurial community was no capitalist free-for-all. It was a federation of wealthy families and their friends.

All of this points to stability in the upper reaches of the Rochester economy. Stability, however, implies continuity over time, and a full 45 percent of the 1827 elite either died or left Rochester within the next ten years. Some—notably Abelard Reynolds and William Atkinson—are known to have failed at least once. And Josiah Bissell poured his fortune into a Sabbath-keeping line of stages and packet boats and died a pious bankrupt in 1831.[29] But despite the ups and downs of individual members, the elite families of 1827 retained continuous control over the Rochester economy. Of those who

stayed in Rochester between 1827 and 1837, 71 percent remained among the richest tenth of property holders. These
accounted for 41 percent of the 1837 elite. Twenty-three percent of the others were their sons, brothers, and in-laws; 7
percent were their business partners. Thus all but 29 percent
of the 1837 elite were tied by blood, marriage, or business
association to men who had held that status ten years earlier
—and this over a boom-and-bust decade that saw the population shoot from 9,000 to 18,000 persons. The continuity
stretched unbroken from the beginnings of settlement. In 1837
four of Rochester's five richest men were sons and sons-in-law
of the original proprietors of 1815.[30]

ROADS TO RICHES

What, then, of the fabled individualism and instability of
Jacksonian society? Rochester folklore is filled with poor boys
who wandered into town in the early years and finished their
lives in mansions. No doubt local patriots romanticized these
stories, but they did not make them up. For among the ten
richest men in Rochester in 1827 there were two who had
grown up amid poverty and/or extreme and repeated economic insecurity. There was indeed room at the top. Thomas
Kempshall and Abelard Reynolds were poor boys who found
it.

The father of Abelard Reynolds was a farmer and sometime
saddler who went broke in at least seven New York and Connecticut towns before his son was eighteen years old.[31] When
Abelard reached his twentieth birthday the family was living
(and failing again) in Windsor, Connecticut. He obtained his
father's permission and traveled to the home of Eliphalet
Wells in Vermont. Wells was no stranger. Years earlier he had
worked as a journeyman saddler and lived in the Reynolds
household. Abelard became a journeyman and then a partner
in the Vermont saddlery, and after a year he left with his first

hundred dollars. On the way home he stopped in Massachusetts and made a down payment on a farm. Then he moved his parents to the farm and went to New Haven with his mother, where they borrowed the rest of the money from his uncles. Abelard finished that year on the new farm, helping his parents establish their first stable home. Then he left permanently. It was 1807 and he was twenty-two years old.

Sometime that year Abelard Reynolds opened a saddlery in Pittsfield, Massachusetts. His activities there are obscure until 1809, when he married a daughter of King Strong and joined one of Pittsfield's first families. He stayed two more years, then roamed through New York and Ohio looking for opportunities to suit an ambitious and now well-connected young man. On the return trip, he stopped at the falls of the Genesee and visited Enos Stone, who was tending his farm and acting as agent for Nathaniel Rochester. It was Stone who talked Reynolds, an old Berkshire County neighbor, into settling at the falls, and it seems to have been Stone who introduced him to Colonel Rochester. Reynolds must have impressed the colonel at their first meeting in 1812. For in that year Rochester used his influence with his former business partner Thomas Hart and with Hart's son-in-law Henry Clay to secure the appointment of Reynolds as the first postmaster of the village. Nine years later the colonel still recognized him as a close friend of the family, and Reynolds never strayed far from the Rochester connection.[32] He and four of the colonel's sons and sons-in-law helped found the Masonic Lodge in the village, and Reynolds sat as director of the Bank of Rochester while it was under Rochester family control.[33] In 1825 he was the Rochester faction's successful candidate for New York assemblyman. Speculating wisely in west-side land and investing the profits in a four-story office building and hotel, this bankrupt saddler's son became one of the richest men in Rochester. But there was nothing of the *arriviste* about Abelard Reynolds. Beginning at the bottom of village society, he knew how to function at the top: as Methodist trustee, as bank director, as Master Mason, as faction politician, and as the husband of a wealthy woman and the father of wealthy children. For Reynolds's individual fortune was inseparable from the social system in which it was made, and from the values and social skills that had won him entry into that system.

Another "self-made" member of the elite was Thomas Kempshall.[34] Kempshall was not only poor but (to complete a mythmaker's dream) an immigrant and an orphan as well. His family came from England and settled ten miles east of the falls in 1806. The father died that year. The oldest son, Willis, found homes for his nine brothers and sisters, then walked to the falls and found work as a carpenter for the Brown brothers. Once established, he sent for his brother Thomas. Thomas worked with Willis, then was placed as a clerk in Ira West's dry-goods store. (It is difficult to determine how this relationship began, but it is noteworthy that both Ira West and Willis Kempshall were Masons.) Kempshall worked hard and learned the business, and in 1823 West took him in as a full partner. When his patron retired the next year, Kempshall bought the business and went into partnership with John Bush, who had clerked the previous two years for Kempshall and West. By 1824 Thomas Kempshall was a man with a future. And like Abelard Reynolds, he took on the life style and responsibilities of a man of property. In that year he married a sister of Everard Peck, a wealthy publisher and speculator from Hartford, and his fellow communicants at St. Luke's Church elected him vestryman. He and John Bush continued to operate their dry-goods store and opened a large mill-furnishing and millstone factory in the second ward. In 1827, as the junior partner of Ebenezer Beach, he built the largest flour mill in the United States.[35] Eleven years later he took a seat in Congress.

For these men, entry into the elite hinged on participation in the elite social world and acceptance within it, and mobility in boom-town Rochester had a peculiarly "sponsored" character.[36] Even the most spectacular leaps between social strata posed no threat to the elite or to established ways of doing things at the top of society. Nor did successful participation in the economy isolate the new rich from their own families and former friends. Abelard Reynolds surrounded himself with one of the most elaborate clans in Rochester. When he held the first Methodist services at his house in 1818, the congregation included his father and sister, who had followed him out of Massachusetts. Before long, his sister-in-law Mary Strong came from Pittsfield and married a son of Matthew Brown, and another of his wife's sisters married into the mill-owning Gibbs family.[37] Reynolds sat at the center of a family network that joined his humble past and his prosperous present, and—when his son opened an extensive seed and farm supplies house in Reynolds Arcade—he passed his good fortune on to a new generation. Thomas Kempshall, the immigrant boy turned miller and congressman, also had company at the top. His dry-goods store stood a few doors from the central corner of Buffalo and State. Next door stood printing offices owned by his in-laws Everard and Jesse Peck, and on the other side was the largest hat factory in western New York, owned and operated by his brothers, Willis and Timothy Kempshall.[38] A successful man in Rochester seldom left his relatives and friends behind, for the economy tended to select kin groups and social networks rather than individuals for success.

The presence of Kempshall and Reynolds among the town's ten richest men suggests that the rags-to-riches story was acted out with considerable frequency. It is the related assumption that the entrepreneurial world was filled with freely competing individualists that must be set aside. Neither of these men made himself. No doubt both were ambitious and talented, but talent and ambition were of no use without the cooperation and patronage of other men. Abelard Reynolds's road to riches led first to one of his father's former employees, then to his uncles in New Haven, his father-in-law in Pittsfield, a wealthy old neighbor who had settled at Rochester, and finally to Colonel Rochester himself—and thence to the immense group resources of the Rochester connection. Neither is it difficult to pinpoint the time at which Thomas Kempshall's fortunes turned for the better. It was his employment and subsequent sponsorship by Ira West. Kempshall's biographer knew that, and he concluded his success story with an odd mix of rugged individualism and a recognition of the importance of friendships with powerful men. "The orphan boy of a foreign emigrant, thrown upon his own resources, unaided but by the patron who had the discrimination to discover merit . . ."[39]

CAPITALISM, MOBILITY, AND THE ROCHESTER REVIVAL

When asked to explain nineteenth-century revivals, most historians point to social dislocations that attended migration and the expansion of the market after 1790. Young persons dissolved old social ties and worked out their careers far from home, and each was forced to create an identity and a system of ethics pretty much out of whole cloth. The result was a nationwide epidemic of unregulated greed, family collapse, adolescent trauma, status anxiety, cultural confusion, simple loneliness, and—as a result—revival religion. To use an older and more cheerful phrase, revivals were society's antidote to individualism.[40] A systematic test of that proposition is long overdue.

Precisely how could individualism translate into religious tension? In Tocqueville's America, the great concomitant of individualism was movement: migration from place to place in search of opportunity, and mobility between social strata once it was found. And mobility is migration between social worlds. A man who moves from one place to another separates himself from the family and neighbors with whom he grew up and in collaboration with whom he arrived at his system of values and his personal identity. Even if he stays at home, vertical mobility creates psychic distance from former intimates who move in different directions or at different speeds. Among migrants and the newly successful (or newly failed), old values are challenged every day. Norms and conceptions of self formulated in another world become alien and oddly unreal, generating confusion and personal anxiety that are often resolved in religious ways.[41] The religious potential of individualism and spatial and occupational mobility lies in their tendency (to borrow a phrase from Tocqueville's followers) to atomize society and thus to deprive people of old ways of understanding themselves and their places in the world.

Rochester was America's first inland boom town, certainly a good place to look for normless men on the make. Few Rochester entrepreneurs, however, fit that description. And if we limit attention to men who joined churches during Charles Finney's revival, we shall find even fewer for whom migration and participation in the entrepreneurial world had been an isolating or norm-shattering experience. More than others, Finney's converts were firmly engaged in the country trade and in the elaborate and stability-inducing relationships through which it was conducted.

Take the case of migration. In 1830 every adult in the city had come from some other place, and no doubt many moved too quickly and too often to maintain stable relationships with kinfolk or anyone else. The Protestant churches, however, formed remarkably stable islands within this shifting population. Both before and during the revival, churches were filled disproportionately with businessmen and master craftsmen and their families—persons who enjoyed far greater residential stability than did other elements of the Rochester population (Table 1).[42] More revealing, the men who joined churches during the Finney revival were more stable than were others even in the same stability-prone occupations—and this despite their relative youth.[43] Anyone wishing to ascribe the Rochester revival to rootlessness must explain the fact that Finney's converts were the most firmly rooted men in town.

TABLE 1. PERSISTENCE OF CHURCHGOING AND NON-CHURCHGOING BUSINESSMEN, PROFESSIONALS, AND MASTER CRAFTSMEN, 1830–1834*

	N	persistence, 1830–34
church member in 1829	60	81
revival convert	62	79
non-church member	104	67

*Includes persons who were businessmen, professionals, and master craftsmen in 1827, and who appear in the 1830 census. For the derivation of occupations, see Appendix A.

Nor had they left their relatives and friends at home. More than others, they came to Rochester in the company of fathers, uncles, and adult brothers, and they made their money in close and continuous collaboration with members of their families. We have seen that illustrated in the careers of Rochester land speculators and of Abelard Reynolds and Thomas Kempshall —all of them Protestant church members. We see it again in Table 2, which describes partnerships formed by Rochester entrepreneurs in the 1820s. The data are rough and incomplete, for family relationships are inferred from surnames.[44] The table is useful, not as an absolute measure, but as a means of comparing patterns of cooperation among three groups of entrepreneurs: those who were church members in 1829, those who joined churches during the revival, and those who never joined a Rochester church. The results are clear. Churchgoing merchants and masters tended to be the proprietors of family firms. Charles Finney's converts entered partnerships with members of their families twice as frequently as did proprietors who stayed outside the churches. The converts were successful men. And like other nineteenth-century businessmen, they stayed in one place and maintained strong ties with relatives.[45] Insofar as there was a relationship between revival religion and mobility and its attendant social isolation, it was demonstrably negative.

TABLE 2. PARTNERSHIPS FORMED BY CHURCHGOING AND NON-CHURCHGOING BUSINESSMEN, PROFESSIONALS, AND MASTER CRAFTSMEN, 1821–29 (PERCENTAGES)

	N	single owner	family partnership	other partnership
church member in 1829	79	41	30	29
revival convert	67	51	27	22
non-church member	175	55	13	32

SOURCES: The table includes all persons who were businessmen, professionals, or master craftsmen in 1827. Partnerships were gathered from newspaper advertisements, tax records, and newspaper notices of the formation and dissolution of partnerships.

Of course family partnerships and residential stability are not proof that Finney's converts had avoided the moral dangers of Jacksonian capitalism. It is possible that they stayed in Rochester and cooperated with brothers and brothers-in-law, and still abandoned the standards of right behavior that they had learned in their home villages. That, however, is unlikely. For the entrepreneurs in Finney's audience seem to have been precisely those who were directly dependent on the countryside. Their livelihoods hinged not only on cunning and business acumen but on reputations for honesty and reliability, and on conformity to the cultural and behavioral norms of rural western New York. Among such men, ungoverned ambition was a fatal liability.

The relation between church membership and involvement in the country trade cannot be documented systematically, for it is impossible to determine the clientele served by most businessmen. But it is clear that men who were independent of the countryside and its moral judgments spent less time in church than those who were not. Most Rochesterians were laborers and journeyman craftsmen, and few of them went to church. Neither did the grocers and boardinghouse keepers who operated businesses in their neighborhoods. These men were relatively poor, and we might conclude that the churches were filled with rich men regardless of their economic functions. But even wealthy entrepreneurs who were independent of the country trade stayed away from church. Forwarding merchants and hotel owners, for instance, were attached to the canal rather than to the farms. Finney touched a few of them, but the vast majority remained outside the churches throughout the 1820s and 1830s.[46] The evangelist drew most of his audience from among the millers, merchants, master craftsmen, and county-seat lawyers who had filled the churches since the beginnings of settlement—men who with few exceptions derived their livings from the country trade.

But perhaps the most telling evidence of ties between the churches and the countryside was the revival itself. Finney made repeated forays into the hinterland, and the revival spread quickly into the surrounding counties. Hundreds of farm families participated in the Rochester meetings, often at the invitation of relatives and friends in the city. And at the height of the excitement Finney had the help of nine ministers from the surrounding countryside. Two of these stayed on to accept Rochester pulpits.[47] The revival did not derive from the problems of ambitious men who had moved to the city and then lost their moral bearings. On the contrary, the revival reaffirmed the moral unity shared throughout the 1820s and 1830s by Genesee farmers and the more prosperous members of the Rochester business community. Whatever generated religious troubles for merchants and masters, it had little to do with rootlessness, isolation, and anomie.

2
Society

ROCHESTER retained the economic functions and much of the look and feel of a country town. But market operations that stabilized the business community in the 1820s filled the streets and workshops with the fastest-growing population in the United States. Many were transients on their way farther west. But most lived and worked in Rochester, creating a bottom-heavy and unstable urban population. In 1827 only 21 percent of adult male Rochesterians were independent proprietors. The others worked for them. Twenty-six percent of the work force possessed no particular skill and looked for casual work along the canal, around the mills and loading docks, and in the streets. But by far the largest group —45 percent—was made up of the journeyman craftsmen who built the town and filled its bulging workshops.[1] In 1830 three-fourths of the population was under thirty years of age. And in the prime working ages of twenty through fifty, the population was overwhelmingly male, suggesting that accounts which described Rochester workmen as young, unattached drifters were not far from accurate.[2] Perhaps most unsettling, these men moved too fast to be counted. In 1826 an editor estimated that 120 persons left Rochester every day, while 130 more arrived to take their places. Of the hundreds of wage earners living in Rochester in 1827, fewer than one in six would stay as long as six years.[3] Near the bottom, the population of Rochester changed constantly.

Few American communities—certainly none in which

Rochester businessmen had lived—had ever held such a young, unstable, and poor population. Day laborers and journeyman craftsmen made up 71 percent of the adult male work force. In Philadelphia, as late as 1820, the comparable figure was 39 percent.[4] Rochester may have looked like a country town. But underneath, it was a blue-collar city. When Charles Finney arrived late in 1830, he found merchants and master workmen at the top of a city that they owned but could not control. The following pages trace their loss of dominance into three closely related spheres: the organization of work, relations between work and family life, and the changing spatial organization of the town.

WORK

The loss of social control began, paradoxically, with the imposition of new and tighter controls over the process of labor. For while market operations revolutionized the scale and intensity of work, they freed wage earners from the immediate discipline exerted by older, household-centered relations of production. Shoe factories, cooperages, and building crews are among the operations for which that process can be documented in some detail. Briefly, here is what happened to the organization of work in those trades.

We begin with shoemaking, one of the key links in Rochester's relations with the countryside. Hides came down the Genesee and were tanned and fabricated into shoes for sale back to the farmers. The earliest shops were small and concentrated on custom work. But within a few years shoemakers were serving a broad regional market. In 1821 a master shoemaker boasted that he was "constantly adding to the number of his workmen" and that he could satisfy not only retail customers but "any store in the state, west of Albany."[5] The 1827 directory listed 111 journeyman shoemakers, most of whom seem to have worked in a few large establishments.

Jesse Hatch counted nine shops that combined shoemaking and retailing in 1831, and left a description of the one in which he found work:

> It was customary for the boss, with the younger apprentices, to occupy the room in front where, with bared arms and leather aprons, they performed their work and met their customers. A shop in the rear or above would be occupied by the tramping journeyman and the older apprentice . . . The shops were low rooms in which from fifteen to twenty men worked . . . [6]

In the earliest shops, masters had hired few helpers. Shoemaking and retailing were performed in the same room and by the same men. But Hatch's employer dealt personally only with his customers and with a few of his younger employees, and it is doubtful that he spent much time making shoes. The front and back rooms had become very different kinds of space.

A newer form, which came to dominate the trade in the late 1820s and early 1830s, completed the separation of men who made shoes from those who sold them. Now masters kept only a foreman and a few trusted employees in the shop. These fitted customers, rough-cut the uppers, and sent them by runner to shoemakers' boardinghouses that dotted back streets in the downtown area. There journeymen shaped and finished the parts. Runners took these to the homes of women who sewed shoes together, then brought the finished product back to the store. The timing of this change is unclear, and certainly it varied from shop to shop. Hatch remembered that in 1831 "most of the work" was done in boardinghouses.[7] In 1834 Rachel Gibson worked as a shoe binder on Mechanic Street. Three doors down lived James Piersons, a runner. Neither occupation was represented in the directory published seven years earlier. At the same time, the proportion of journeymen who lived in boardinghouses doubled. By the early 1830s the business of selling shoes was separate from the act of making them. Control over the trade fell from shoemakers to the merchant capitalists (many of them former shoemakers), who arranged the purchase of raw materials, organized the cheap and rapid production of shoes, and marketed the finished product.

The separation of proprietor from wage earner took place more quickly among coopers. Coopers' shops were ancillary to flour mills that used hundreds of thousands of barrels annually. The two largest shops were owned by the millers Matthew Brown and Harvey Ely, and operated as parts of their mills. Steady markets and high profits encouraged other businessmen to invest in cooperages. The realtors Bradford and Moses King and the publisher Luther Tucker were among those who went into the business of making barrels.[8] And of the shop owners listed as coopers, some spent their time doing other things. The directory described Pierce Darrow as a cooper. One of the larger proprietors, he called himself a lumber merchant.[9] Probably it was a better description of what he did. Flour barrels were produced in huge quantities, and they did not have to be as tight and well made as kegs and barrels that held liquid. Coopers did little more than assemble staves that were pre-cut up the valley. A skilled craft had become linked with extensive and unified business operations, and there was little employment in Rochester for men who knew how to make fine barrels. It is noteworthy that this was one of the few skilled trades that employed significant numbers of blacks—men who with few exceptions concentrated in the least desirable kinds of work.[10]

By far the largest group of Rochester workingmen was engaged in building the town itself. Rochester was the fastest-growing city in the United States, and carpenters seldom contracted for individual houses as they had in older and more slowly growing communities. The need for housing produced a uniform two-story, four-room house (whitewashed and trimmed in dark green) that was duplicated endlessly across the landscape. During the building season of 1827, Rochester builders put up 352 new houses.[11] That was about one and a half houses per carpenter in the space of a few months. An editor marveled at the number of "frames" being raised, suggesting that these were cheap and easily constructed balloon-frame houses, put up quickly by large groups of men. They did not have to custom-fit doors and window frames, for Silas Hawley—with the help of two sons, three journeymen, and a roomful of water-driven machinery—turned out thousands of them in uniform sizes.[12] Building crews worked in gangs supervised by foremen and subcontractors, and the men who organized the operation and sold the finished houses were as often as not land speculators. Nathaniel Rochester, for instance, built and owned scores of houses all over town. So did others whose occupations were listed as merchant, miller, realtor—even shoemaker.[13] Like coopers and shoemakers, Rochester building tradesmen worked for men they seldom saw.

These three trades were controlled by merchant capitalists, men more skilled at organizing and driving workers and selling what they made than at making things themselves.[14] In each trade the result was a dilution of traditional skills, an expansion in the size of work groups, and the making of a lot of money by men who controlled the operation. There were similar developments among metal workers, tailors, hatters, clothiers, and boat builders.[15] Many other crafts that did not come under the direct control of merchant capitalists were ancillary to their operations. Lastmakers and pegmakers were subsidiary to the shoe trade. Brickmakers, paint mixers, and nailers produced for master builders. In most manufacturing operations, the greatest rewards went to masters who turned themselves into businessmen—or to men who had never been masters at all.

While most wage earners came under the ultimate control of merchant capitalists, changes in the pace, scale, and organization of work varied enormously from trade to trade. Some coopers escaped change altogether. The smallest shops were owned by Irishmen who refused to alter the customs of their trade, and throughout the 1820s and 1830s, coopers in the fifth-ward neighborhood known as Dublin spent Sundays drunk and Mondays visiting their friends, sharpening their tools, and clearing their heads. From Tuesday on, they worked relentlessly to deliver barrels to the mills on time.[16] (No doubt coopers directly attached to the mills experienced more regular and more harassing forms of discipline.) Shoemakers in the boardinghouses were also free to work in spurts and at irregular times—again, as long as they met insistent deadlines. Shoemaking was quiet and sedentary, and the men read aloud, gambled, told stories, and debated endlessly.[17] Carpenters had the worst of it. They labored from sunrise to sunset under the eyes of men who contracted to build scores of houses over a short season, and the work was unremitting. Unable to control their conditions of work or to mix work and leisure, they organized to limit the time that they spent on the job. In 1834 journeyman carpenters struck for a ten-hour day, and announced wearily that "we will be faithful to our employers during the ten hours and no longer."[18]

But while circumstances varied, journeymen all over the city experienced harsher, more impersonal, and more transparent forms of exploitation than had men in the same trades a few years earlier. At the same time they were freed from controls imposed by the smaller workshops, for the businessmen who bought and controlled their labor were seldom present when the work was performed. They worked together and talked and joked among themselves, and they forged sensibilities that were specific to the class of wage-earning craftsmen. Basic to that mental set was the proposition that master and wage earner were different and opposed kinds of men. In 1829 an editor had occasion to use the word boss, and followed it with an asterisk. "A foreman or master workman," he explained. "Of modern coinage, we believe."[19] Five years later the striking carpenters used the word again. This time, there was no asterisk.[20]

HOUSEHOLDS

The reorganization of work brought change into the most intimate corners of daily life. For until the coming of merchant capitalism, most Rochester wage earners lived with their employers and shared in their private lives. Evidence is fragmentary and incomplete, and quantifiable data are unavailable, but this much is clear: in 1820 merchants and master workmen lived above, behind, or very near their places of business, and employees boarded in their homes. On most jobs, employment was conditional on co-residence. Even workmen whose fathers and brothers headed households in Rochester lived with employers.[21] Work, leisure, and domestic life were acted out in the same place and by the same people, and relations between masters and men transferred without a break from the workshop to the fireside.

In traditional usage the word family, with all that it implied, stretched to include co-resident employees. When the publisher Everard Peck married in 1820, his wife spent weeks setting up a new household, then wrote home: "We collected our family together which consists of seven persons and we think ourselves pleasantly situated."[22] How newlyweds—both of them marrying for the first time—had gathered such a large family must remain a mystery. But some of those seven almost certainly worked for Everard Peck. (In 1827 the Peck household included Everard and his wife and children, his brother and business partner Jesse, a day laborer, and four journeyman printers and bookbinders.) Peck took these men into his home knowing that he owed them more than room and board. He assured his father-in-law that

> We cannot be too frequently or too forcibly reminded of the responsibility under which we are placed, to discharge faithfully the important trust committed to our charge. Although we are conscious that we fall short of discharging our duty to each other and to those who are placed in our family and under our care we have not been we hope altogether unmindful of it.

> Our own happiness, the welfare of those connected with us, and the harmony and good order of our family, doubtless depend very much on the manner in which we commence our new course in life.[23]

Puritan family government was in decay, but it still ranked high in Rochester Protestants' ideas of where authority was located and how it should be exercised. Wage earners were young and poor and numerous. Left alone, they might cause trouble. But with each of them a member of some household, and with householders answerable for the behavior of everyone under their care, the community could breathe easy.[24] Public opinion held heads of families accountable for what their "children and dependents" did. So did New York law, and a justice of the peace threatened to take legal action when he spied a group of boys and young men skating on Sunday, "to the great shame and disgrace of their parents and masters."[25] For those who attended Presbyterian and Baptist churches, religious sanctions reinforced custom, law, and watchful neighbors. The covenant at First Presbyterian Church reminded householders that they were "under solemn obligations to restrain their children and dependents . . . from all sinful and unlawful amusements," and to enforce their attendance at church. The rules of practice at Second Church, drawn up at the height of the boom in 1825, repeated those admonitions.[26] A year later Robert Willson, the town's wealthiest master builder, shared his house with five journeyman carpenters and, according to one of his neighbors, "took an interest in the conduct of all the young men he employed."[27] As late as 1828, a businessman reaffirmed the belief that "every habitual sin openly practised in the family, by any of its members, is justly chargeable upon its head." (He gave this as one of his reasons for denying drinks to his workmen. The result was that "their work has been better done, and my family more quiet and orderly.")[28] The tradition that a man's responsibility for the welfare and behavior of his wife and children extended to whoever else slept beneath his roof came to Rochester with the first settlers. If we may believe these pious men, it remained strong for many years.

But even as merchants and masters talked of patriarchy, the intimacy on which it depended fell apart. Everard Peck was co-publisher of a small weekly newspaper when he established his household in 1820. By 1830 he operated printing offices and a daily paper, a bookstore, a paper mill and warehouse, and speculated extensively in Rochester real estate. While he continued to board employees, his attention was engaged in operations that went beyond relations with young printers and bookbinders. The same subtle estrangement was occurring in stores and workshops all over Rochester. And in more and more cases, the change was not so subtle: workmen were leaving the homes of their employers.

The first opportunity to view that process comes with the Rochester Directory of 1827. That document lists the names, residences, and occupations of males over the age of sixteen. Boarders appear beside their landlords, permitting a reconstruction of the adult male membership of households in 1827. The figures are incomplete, for they exclude women and children. Domestic servants and the younger apprentices and clerks are lost from view, and there were many of these. Simeon Allcott's cotton factory and the tannery operated by Samuel Works and Jacob Graves hired large numbers of children. (Both expressed regrets when young workers were sucked into their machinery and killed.[29]) Work crews in the larger shoe shops included four or five apprentices, and there are enough advertisements for apprentices, notices of runaways, and wringing of hands over the moral state of apprentices and clerks to suggest that children participated in most economic operations. Servant girls, apprentices, and clerks lived where they worked. Figures that exclude them seriously underestimate the number of wage earners living with their employers. But the households of Rochester proprietors were crowded nonetheless.

Fifty-two percent of master craftsmen and 39 percent of merchants and professionals included adult male wage earners in their households in 1827. But these bulging families housed only a small proportion of Rochester workingmen. The large number of lodgers—overwhelmingly wage earners—in households headed by laborers and journeymen points to that fact. So does the prevalence of boarders in the homes of shopkeepers and petty proprietors, many of whom were grocers who rented beds to workmen.[30] In all, 37 percent of journeymen headed their own households. Twenty-nine percent of the others boarded with them. Another 11 percent slept in boardinghouses and groceries, leaving only 22 percent in households headed by employers.[31] The custom of providing room and board as part of a workman's wages was alive in 1827. But it certainly was in decay.

Proprietors in 1827 were in transit between family-centered work relations and pure wage labor. A second directory appeared in 1834. Reliable lists of masters in that year can be compiled only for shoemakers and proprietors of a variety of small indoor workshops, and in some ways that is a happy limitation. Merchant capitalists were in firm control of the shoe trade by 1834, and the organization of work among shoemakers changed dramatically. The shops averaged nine journeymen, and sometimes had more than twenty. But among tinsmiths, sashmakers, gunsmiths, printers, and the like, work groups remained small. In many cases the master still worked beside his employees. Thus these two groups represent extremes in the development of Rochester manufactures. In 1827 only one in four shoemakers but almost half the small-shop craftsmen lived with proprietors in their trades. Living arrangements for both groups, however, headed in the same direction. By 1834 the figure for live-in shoemakers had dropped to one in twenty; for small-shop craftsmen to one in three.[32] Even wage earners who continued to receive room and board from their employers sometimes received it in peculiar ways. A young man who clerked in a downtown dry-goods store in 1828 remembered sleeping on a cot in the back room, surrounded by barrels and packing crates. His employer, assured that the store was being watched at night, slept with his family on a quiet side street.[33]

Rochester merchants and masters had grown up in communities in which labor relations and family life were structurally and emotionally inseparable. Most had served resident clerkships and apprenticeships, some of them in Rochester itself.[34] But in the 1820s the nature of work and of the work force made it difficult to provide employees with food, lodgings, behavioral models. and domestic discipline. Even proprietors who kept employees in their homes (and these tended more and more to be the youngest apprentices and clerks) often retained customary forms while neglecting the responsibilities that had given them meaning. An editor addressed these questions to the town's churchgoing businessmen:

> Have apprentices and clerks immortal souls? Are their masters, or employers, being professed Christians, to be considered as having charge of those souls? Is prayer, and especially family prayer, one of the means of grace? Are those masters or employers, being professors of religion, doing their duty, who keep their apprentices or clerks in the shop, or store, during the time of family worship, when those apprentices and clerks reside in, and are members of the family? These apprentices and clerks, being excluded from *family* prayer, is there not reason to fear they are also forgotten in *secret* devotion? May not these questions furnish one reason why there are so many ungodly clerks and apprentices in our country?[35]

Certainly Rochester had its share of ungodly young employees. And men who had abdicated immediate, personal responsibility for their spiritual state could blame no one but themselves.

NEIGHBORHOODS

In 1820 most Rochesterians worked, played, and slept in the same place. There were no neighborhoods as we understand them: no distinct commercial and residential zones, no residential areas based upon social class. The integration of work and family life and of master and wage earner produced a nearly random mix of people and activities on the city's streets. That changed quickly after 1825. Masters moved their families away from their places of business, and some of the side streets took on a distinctive middle-class, residential character. Workingmen, freed from their employers' households, moved into neighborhoods of their own. Within a few short years, the transformation of work and the estrangement of master from wage earner were recapitulated in the social geography of Rochester.

Maps 1 and 2 trace that development between 1827 and 1834. On those maps, the streets that formed the Four Corners (Buffalo, Main, State, and Exchange) are termed the central business district. This included nearly all stores and offices and most of the larger workshops that were not powered by water.[36] Other streets are classified by the proportions of wage earners and proprietors who lived on them, computed from samples that include all businessmen, professionals, and master workmen, all day laborers, and all journeyman shoemakers and small-shop craftsmen—exclusive of those who boarded with their employers. This population includes roughly equal numbers of Rochester's richest and poorest men. Streets on which proprietors accounted for 70 percent or more of sample residents are termed middle-class residential. Those with between 30 and 69 percent proprietors are mixed residential, and

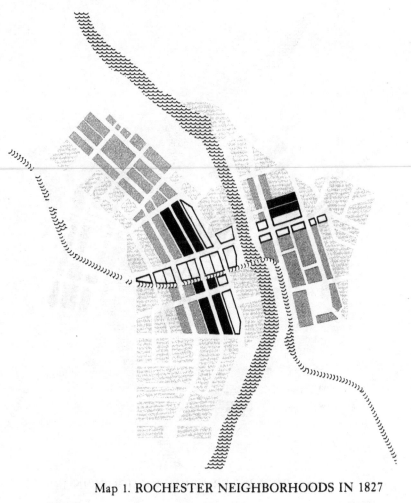

Map 1. ROCHESTER NEIGHBORHOODS IN 1827

Central Business District

Middle-Class Residential

Mixed Residential

Working-Class Residential

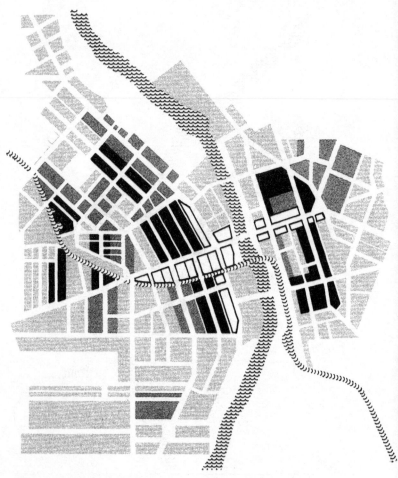

Map 2. ROCHESTER NEIGHBORHOODS IN 1834

☐ Central Business District

■ Middle-Class Residential

▨ Mixed Residential

▒ Working-Class Residential

those with fewer than 30 percent proprietors are working-class residential. All but a few streets ended or changed names within two blocks. Thus these figures map the demography of social class block by block; it is a map that changed dramatically between 1827 and 1834.[37]

In 1827 the English traveler Basil Hall sat at his window in the Eagle Tavern and sketched the buildings running east from the courthouse square on Buffalo Street. They included a cabinet factory, a grocery, a painter's shop, a provisions store, and a shoe factory. Each of them was a modest, two-story wooden structure, and each had what appears to have been living space on the second floor.[38] Masters and merchants used those rooms. Fully 37 percent of business-owning families resided—presumably at or near their places of business—on the busiest downtown streets. So did 31 percent of journeymen and laborers. The town's central intersection remained mixed commercial, manufacturing, residential, and recreational space.

The side streets on which the remaining two-thirds of Rochesterians lived were as thoroughly mixed as the Four Corners. Residents of even the wealthiest blocks walked out of their houses to find a cross section of the city. Deacon Oren Sage of the Baptist Church, for instance, owned a house at the corner of Fitzhugh and Ann. In the mornings he walked down the most uniformly wealthy street in Rochester. But tucked between the homes of merchants and manufacturers were four households headed by day laborers, two headed by journeyman shoemakers, another headed by a printer, and two workingmen's boardinghouses. Along with these came a variety of nonresidential establishments. The Quaker Meetinghouse was across the street from Sage's home, and sprinkled down the block were a bakery owned by a family of former slaves, a combined tailor's shop and neighborhood bar, Brick Presbyterian Church, a livery stable with a carriage factory upstairs, and the Monroe County Jail.[39] Deacon Sage stepped from

North Fitzhugh onto Buffalo Street and found only a noisier and more crowded part of the remarkably undifferentiated space in which he worked and made his home.

We cannot, however, view neighborhoods at only one point in time, for the integration of social classes and of economic and domestic activities was breaking down in the late 1820s. The change was dramatized in 1828 with the opening of Reynolds Arcade on Buffalo Street. That building provided four stories of office space to businessmen and professionals, all of whom lived someplace else. Across the river the Globe Building rented water-powered workrooms to at least fifteen manufacturers—again, without living space. By 1834 Buffalo and Main and the major artery that crossed them west of the river presented a continuous line of brick store fronts. The business district stood nearly empty at night: only 15 percent of proprietors continued to live on those streets. Masters had separated their families from their work, and there is evidence that the change was bound up with a new concern for privacy. Even men who still lived and worked in the same place found ways to create distinct domestic territory. Many lawyers, for instance, kept offices in their homes. In 1834 they announced that they did not wish to be bothered before nine in the morning or after five in the evening. While it remained convenient to combine economic and family space, they had apparently determined to separate economic from domestic time.[40]

Business-owning families were in retreat from the world of work, and from the increasingly distinct world of workingmen. By 1834 the middle class concentrated off Buffalo in the first and third wards and on North St. Paul and Clinton Streets on the east side. Workingmen disappeared from those streets. On South Fitzhugh the number of wage earners dropped from five to none; on North Sophia from twenty to six; on South Clinton from nine to two; on North Fitzhugh from seven to two (the boardinghouses, the bakery, the tailor's shop and bar, and the county jail had also disappeared). Workmen still clustered near the center of town—on Mechanic and Water Streets, in the mixed manufacturing and residential jumble of South St. Paul, and in alleys throughout the downtown area. But they dispersed more and more toward the outskirts: in Dublin, in the Cornhill section of the third ward, and in the tangle of little streets that filled the second ward and sprawled north beyond the city limits. It was the classic spatial pattern of nineteenth-century cities.[41]

By 1834 the social geography of Rochester was class-specific: master and wage earner no longer lived in the same households or on the same blocks. But except at the outskirts, no class could claim regions of the city as its own. Nearly every family still lived within 750 yards of the Four Corners, and residents of the most exclusive streets could look across their back fences or around the corner and see the new working-class neighborhoods. And every night the sounds of quarrels, shouting, and laughter from the poorer quarters invaded their newly secluded domestic worlds. North St. Paul, for instance, had become an exclusively middle-class enclave on the east side. A few steps toward the river stood Water and Mechanic Streets, a jumble of shacks and cheap rooming houses that made up one of the poorest, noisiest, and most congested areas of Rochester. Towering over this slum, within easy smelling distance of the fine houses on St. Paul, stood one of the largest tanneries in the United States. To the north sprawled Dublin. St. Paul was the only path from there to the downtown jobs and amusements. One wealthy resident remembered coming out of his house on Sunday morning and finding a drunk asleep on the porch.[42]

Across the river, South Fitzhugh Street was now a double row of mansions running off the courthouse square. We may be certain that few of the families on Fitzhugh joined the crowds at the circus on Exchange Street. But they heard clapping and shouting whenever that building was open. Three blocks west of them a fire on Ford Street was attributed to the drunkenness of everyone in the house, while on Troup Street, within easy earshot of Fitzhugh, a gathering of workmen and their families broke into a fight in which a man was stabbed and a woman who ran in to stop it was hit on the breast and bitten badly on the finger.[43] In 1829 Edward Morgan went to jail for operating a gambling room in his house on South Sophia, only a few steps away from the families on Fitzhugh.[44] Grocers on nearby streets were frequently hauled into court for opening their doors and allowing men to drink and make noise on Sunday. Finally, the Erie Canal crossed the northern end of the block. The principal boat basin stood across Exchange, and boats waiting to unload lined the canal as it crossed Fitzhugh. A brawl between rival crews that began at the basin and spilled onto the Four Corners in 1829 was certainly heard if not seen by the people on South Fitzhugh.[45] So were the transgressions of one Erastus Bearcup, a steersman arrested in 1826 for shouting obscenities at ladies on a passing boat.[46]

Across Buffalo, comfortable residents of the first ward and boarders at the prestigious Eagle Tavern contended not only with the poor neighborhoods that surrounded them but with the theater on State Street. Theater crowds were rowdy. During a performance of *Othello*, the manager had to stop the show and plead with the audience to stop shouting and throwing things at the actors. A sleepless editor complained that

> the inhabitants who are so unfortunate as to reside within gunshot of the theatre, have been compelled to hear till midnight or after, reiterated peals of *hooting, howling, shouting, shrieking,* and almost every other unseemly noise, that it is possible for the human gullet to send forth, insomuch that it is next to impossible to obtain repose till the theatrical audience have retired to *their* homes or hovels.[47]

And so on. Businessmen and their families worried incessantly about what went on in the squalid streets and questionable establishments that surrounded their homes. Perhaps the fact that they could hear transgressions but not see them added a touch of menace to what they perceived.

SOCIABILITY: THE CASE OF DRINKING

By 1830 the household economy had all but passed out of existence, and so had the social order that it sustained. Work, family life, the makeup of neighborhoods—the whole pattern of society—separated class from class: master and wage earner inhabited distinct social worlds. Workmen experienced new kinds of harassment on the job. But after work they entered a fraternal, neighborhood-based society in which they were free to do what they wanted. At the same time masters devised standards of work discipline, domestic privacy, and social peace that were directly antithetical to the spontaneous and noisy sociability of the workingmen. The two worlds stood within a few yards of each other, and they fought constantly. That battle took place on many fronts. But from the beginning it centered on alcohol.

The temperance question was nonexistent in 1825. Three years later it was a middle-class obsession.[48] Sullen and disrespectful employees, runaway husbands, paupers, Sabbath breakers, brawlers, theatergoers: middle-class minds joined them in the image of a drink-crazed proletariat. In 1829 the county grand jury repeated what had become, in a remarkably short time, bourgeois knowledge: strong drink was "the cause of almost all of the crime and almost all of the misery that flesh is heir to."[49]

These sentiments were new in the late 1820s. Whiskey was not, and we must ask how liquor became a problem, and particularly how it came to shape perceptions of every other social ill. That search will take us back into workshops, households, and neighborhoods. For working-class drinking and middle-class anxieties about it were bound up with the economic and social transformation of the 1820s. Liquor was indeed a fitting symbol of what had happened: nowhere was the making of distinct classes and the collapse of old social controls dramatized more neatly, more angrily, and in so many aspects of life.

Most temperance advocates had been drinking all their lives, for until the middle 1820s liquor was an absolutely normal accompaniment to whatever men did in groups. Nearly every family kept a bottle in the house to "treat" their guests and workmen, and such community gatherings as election days, militia musters, and Fourth of July celebrations invariably witnessed heavy drinking by men at all levels of society. Merchants who would become temperance spokesmen stocked huge supplies of whiskey, and rich men joined freely in groups where bottles were passed from hand to hand. The flour mills in particular were community gathering places, and farmers waiting to use the mills lounged with the millers and with other local citizens and drank.[50] Among laborers and building tradesmen, the dram was an indispensable part of daily wages. And in the workshops, drinking was universal. Not only independent craftsmen and shoemakers hidden away in boarding-houses, but men who worked directly under churchgoing proprietors drank on the job and with their employers. A store clerk remembered that Edwin Scrantom (he was the editor who expressed concern for unprayed-for apprentices and clerks) "often came into our store for a pitcher of ale to cheer up the boys in the printing offices nearby."[51] Only once in the early years is there record of drinking having caused trouble. In 1818 musicians in the town band—prominent professionals and master craftsmen among them—found themselves too drunk to play. Thereafter, they reduced consumption at rehearsals.[52]

Liquor was embedded in the pattern of irregular work and

easy sociability sustained by the household economy. It was a bond between men who lived, worked, and played together, a compliment to the unique kind of domination associated with that round of life. Workmen drank with their employers, in situations that employers controlled. The informal mixing of work and leisure and of master and wage earner softened and helped legitimate inequality. At the same time drunkenness remained within the bounds of what the master considered appropriate. For it was in his house that most routine drinking was done, and it was he who bought the drinks.

That changed abruptly in the 1820s. Masters increased the pace, scale, and regularity of production, and they hired young strangers with whom they shared no more than contractual obligations. The masters were becoming businessmen, concerned more with the purchase of labor and raw materials and the distribution of finished goods than with production itself. They began to absent themselves from the workshops. At the same time they demanded new standards of discipline and regularity within those rooms. We shall see that those standards included abstinence from strong drink.[53] Now workmen drank less often and less openly on the job. And when they drank, they shared the relaxation and conviviality only with each other, while masters sat in the front room or in another part of town dealing with customers and dreaming up new ways to make things cheaply and quickly.

After work, master and wage earner retreated further into worlds of their own. Masters walked down quiet side streets and entered households that had seceded from the marketplace. Separated from work and workingmen, they and their wives and children turned the middle-class family into a refuge from the amoral economy and disorderly society outside its doors. It was not only the need for clearheaded calculation at work but the new ethos of bourgeois family life that drove businessmen away from the bottle. For unlike the large and public households of 1820, these private little homes—increasingly under the governance of pious housewives—were inappropriate places in which to get drunk. By 1830 the doorway to a middle-class home separated radically different kinds of space: drunkenness and promiscuous sociability on the outside, privacy and icy sobriety indoors.[54]

In the middle and late 1820s whiskey disappeared from settings that the middle class controlled. But in banishing liquor from their workshops and homes, proprietors reached the new limits of what they could in fact control. And it was at those limits that alcohol took on its symbolic force.

Workingmen were building an autonomous social life, and heavy drinking remained part of it. In 1827 Rochester contained nearly 100 establishments licensed to sell drinks. These were not great beer halls and saloons (they would arrive much later in the century) but houses and little businesses where workmen combined drinking with everyday social transactions. On the downtown streets a workman could get a glass of whiskey at groceries, at either of two candy stores, or at a barber shop a few steps from the central business intersection—all of them gathering places for men like himself.[55] At night he could join the crowds at the theater, spending time before and after the show in the noisy and crowded barroom that occupied the basement. On the way home, he would pass the establishments of other licensed grogsellers, for they were everywhere in the workingman's Rochester. The men who operated bars in the poorer neighborhoods shared the sensibilities and many of the experiences of their patrons, for fully 43 percent of them were wage earners themselves. These part-time barkeepers included thirteen journeymen and eight laborers, two boatmen, two teamsters, three clerks, and a pair of schoolteachers. A five-dollar license permitted them to sell drinks, adding to their incomes and fitting their households into the emerging pattern of working-class neighborhood life.

Alongside these kitchen barrooms stood businesses licensed to sell whiskey: food shops and small variety stores, taverns,

and the home workshops of a few of the smaller master craftsmen. These were social centers on a large scale, for many of
them doubled as boardinghouses. Of shopkeepers and petty
proprietors licensed to sell drinks in 1827 (N=23), 52 percent
took in lodgers. (Among the 51 who did not serve drinks, the
comparable figure was 8 percent.)[56] These ramshackle establishments—"disorderly," the newspapers called them—carried on traditions that had been abandoned in the workshops,
maintaining an easy integration of economic, domestic, and
leisure activities, and of life indoors with the life of the neighborhood. Perhaps typical was the bakery run by John C. Stevens on the canal towpath off Exchange Street. During the day
Stevens and his family baked bread. But they stopped at odd
times to serve drinks and talk with canal men and dock workers from the boat basin a few steps away. In the evenings they
were joined by the journeyman carpenter and the school-
teacher who boarded in their home, and by whoever else decided to drop by, and the activities of the household merged
imperceptibly with the flow of neighborhood life.[57]

The Stevens bakery was a lively and crowded place, lively
in a very old way. Merchants and masters might peer down the
towpath and see that functions they once performed—the pro-
vision of food and a place to sleep, whiskey and the companionship and relaxation that went with it—were being taken up
by workingmen themselves, or by such questionable proprietors as John C. Stevens. It gave the old family governors something to ponder as they disappeared into their own secluded
homes.

The link between drinking and violence was, of course,
more than a figment of middle-class imaginations. Alcohol was
surrounded by new, perhaps looser cultural controls. At the
same time, workingmen experienced punishing changes in
what they could expect from life, and some social drinkers
took a turn toward the pathological. The laborer who stabbed
a friend in 1828, the boat carpenter who beat a workmate to

death with a calking mallet in 1829, and the man who killed his wife in the middle of North St. Paul Street were all drunk and can all, I think, be put into that category.[58] But we must also note that official intervention in working-class neighborhoods—and it came with increasing frequency—sometimes created violence where there had been none. In 1830 a Negro blacksmith turned on the constable who was arresting him for gambling and beat him unconscious. A few months later, neighbors rescued an offender before officials could get him off the block. And in 1833 a constable entered a grocery to quiet a disturbance and was kicked to death.[59] The new neighborhoods were building an independent social life, and some workmen were demonstrating that they would meet outside meddling with force.

The drinking problem of the late 1820s stemmed directly from the new relationship between master and wage earner. Alcohol had been a builder of morale in household workshops, a subtle and pleasant bond between men. But in the 1820s proprietors turned their workshops into little factories, moved their families away from their places of business, and devised standards of discipline, self-control, and domesticity that banned liquor. By default, drinking became part of an autonomous working-class social life, and its meaning changed. When proprietors sent temperance messages into the new neighborhoods, they received replies such as this:

> Who are the most temperate men of modern times? Those who quaff the juice of the grape with their friends, with the greatest good nature, after the manner of the ancient patriarchs, without any malice in their hearts, or the cold-water, pale-faced, money-making men, who make the necessities of their neighbors their opportunity for grinding the face of the poor?[60]

An ancient bond between classes had become, within a very short time, an angry badge of working-class status.

The liquor question dominated social and political conflict in Rochester from the late 1820s onward. At every step, it pitted a culturally independent working class against entrepreneurs who had dissolved the social relationships through which they had controlled others, but who continued to consider themselves the rightful protectors and governors of their city.

3
Politics

ROCHESTER proprietors had migrated from villages in which the public peace was secure. In the villages the more troublesome outsiders and dissidents were expelled. The others were governed by household heads, the disciplinary machinery of the church, and the web of community relationships. But in Rochester in the middle 1820s troublemakers numbered into the hundreds, and they lived outside the families, churches, and social networks that proprietors controlled. There remained one institution with the power to stop them: the village government. In 1826 that body was reorganized and empowered to arrest drunkards and gamblers and to close the theater, the circus, and the dramshops. The new powers, however, were never used. The reasons were twofold. First, the Antimasonic hysteria of 1827 and 1828 divided and destroyed the officeholding elite. Party politicians took their places. Second, voters made it clear that they did not want to be reformed by force. As a result, candidates in the late 1820s stayed away from the questions of temperance and social disorder. Those who did not lost elections, and official power became available only to men who promised not to use it.

FACTIONS

It was Antimasonry that played the greatest part in crippling the elite. The popular attack upon the Masonic Lodge was a strange phenomenon, and it has attracted scholars interested not only in politics but in the irrational and bizarre in social movements.¹ In Rochester, however, Antimasonry made sense. It was a skillfully directed assault upon wealthy and powerful men who had been the focus of resentment since the beginnings of settlement. Antimasons discredited these men and drove them out of politics, leaving a divided and embittered elite to face the social crisis of the late 1820s. An understanding of Antimasonry and of the political paralysis that it helped create begins with the politicians and the political system that Antimasons destroyed.

The Rochester elections of 1817 had stamped the pattern of village politics. The first village president was Francis Brown, who with his brother and cousin and their families had come from Rome, New York, in 1810 to occupy landholdings on the west bank. Accompanying Brown on the first board of trustees were his business partner William Cobb and two close associates of his foreman, Hamlet Scrantom: the master carpenter Daniel Mack, and Jehiel Barnard, who was Scrantom's son-in-law and an old neighbor and friend of the Browns. The fifth trustee was Everard Peck, whose Federalist and Clintonian newspaper reflected the sentiments of the Brown family connection. Conspicuously absent were the family and friends of Nathaniel Rochester. Apparently his friends had plotted to dominate the village government, had been found out, and had been defeated by the Brown slate of candidates. Rochester wrote asking the rival clan to "heal the wound before it becomes an ulcer," but with little success.² The Browns and their associates dominated town meetings throughout the early and middle 1820s. Francis Brown served three consecutive terms as village president, then turned the job over to his brother Matthew, who served six of the next seven years. The one year in which the Browns did not hold the highest village office was 1824. That year the job went to J. W. Strong, a Clintonian ally who at the time was collaborating with the Browns in one of their bitter disputes with Colonel Nathaniel Rochester.

Although Colonel Rochester and his family never controlled the board of trustees, he stood at the center of village politics. The secret of Rochester's capacity to arouse jealousy and opposition in other rich men lay not in the size and influence of his family or even in his money. It lay in his connections with Martin Van Buren's Bucktail Republican faction at Albany, connections that made the colonel's son William the Bucktail candidate for governor of New York in 1826.[3] Twice during the 1820s, Rochester used those ties to gain spectacular favors for himself and what were considered unfair advantages over other wealthy villagers. Rochester lobbied with the help of his neighbors for the creation of a new county at the mouth of the Genesee in 1821. He received not only the county but had his town named county seat and donated ground on his Hundred-Acre Tract for the county buildings—thus ensuring that land he owned would become the center of a busy town. Francis and Matthew Brown had helped lobby for the county, but they had hoped that their land would become its center. As it turned out, the Browns watched as the fine houses they had built near their proposed civic center were surrounded by the modest homes of journeymen, laborers, and shopkeepers in what became the out-of-the-way second ward.[4]

Rival speculators were angered again when the colonel and his friends began pressuring the legislature to charter a bank in their village. His Clintonian rivals lobbied for a different bank in 1822, and both were refused. The factions joined temporarily and sent Thurlow Weed, the young editor of the Clintonian newspaper, to Albany. Weed successfully negotiated the charter, and the village had a bank in 1824—with Nathaniel Rochester as temporary president. When the directors under his control finished selling stock, it became clear that the Bank of Rochester would be controlled by the Rochester clan and their Bucktail friends in the eastern part of the state. Colonel Rochester had used his connections to gain control of the bank, and thus of the financing of major business operations in his town. This time, Clintonians did not stand

still. Pointing to anti-democratic tendencies of the statewide
Bucktails as well as to the shifty means by which local Buck-
tails had taken over the bank, Clintonians reorganized as the
People's Party and swept the next elections. Within a year,
they had ousted the Bucktail directors and established the
Bank of Rochester as a Clintonian institution.[5]

Rochester politics in the early 1820s were dominated by
feuding between the Rochesters and their Bucktail friends and
a Clintonian faction that revolved around the families of Matthew Brown, J. W. Strong, and Levi Ward. Bucktails, who
called themselves "merchants" at the first town meeting, were
overwhelmingly businessmen and lawyers. Clintonians were
merchants and manufacturers. Both, however, were rich. The
political dividing line was not social class but family jealousies
compounded by religion and geographic origins.[6] Nathaniel
Rochester and his sons were Marylanders, although many of
his associates and distant kin were New Yorkers and New
Englanders. They spent Sunday mornings at St. Luke's Episcopal Church. The colonel had donated the land on which St.
Luke's was built, and he and his family rented the most expensive pews. While his sons and friends served the congregation
as vestrymen, Rochester personally recruited Francis H. Cuming to fill the pulpit. In 1822 the colonel's son Thomas married
Reverand Cuming's sister, making the minister's attachment
to the Rochester clan official.[7]

Clintonians were New Englanders, and the wealthier of
them affiliated with First Presbyterian Church, which stood
across the courthouse square from St. Luke's. The Browns
were at First Church, and their cousin Warren had been
elected elder at the first meeting in 1813. Jacob Gould, who
helped organize the People's campaign, occupied one of the
front pews, as did Levi Ward and his son-in-law Moses Chapin. In the choir, the Clintonian Frederick Backus was bari-
tone soloist.[8] These were leading members of First Church: all
of them natives of New England, and all of them Clintonians.

Even before the fighting started, one of Nathaniel Rochester's partners warned him that "I have learned enough of Yankees to dread & fear their wiles & offers. You are too honest and unsuspicious—take heed my friend or they will be your ruin."[9] Rochester soon had reason to remember the warning.

Factions split the elite along religious and cultural lines, but only because politics was grounded in kinship. At the conclusion of the bank fight Colonel Rochester explained what from his standpoint was the central issue in village politics: ". . . some hotheaded politicians such as Brown, Strong, and others have frequently said that my family had too much influence and must be put down. They have always considered me in their way."[10] This was faction politics, centering on jealousy and competition for honor between a few wealthy gentlemen and their families and friends. Underneath that competition lay an additional and temporarily inoffensive fact: the Rochesters belonged to the Masonic Lodge; their opponents did not.

Late in 1826 there began a series of events that altered the old factions, politicized village government, and made the nastiest of earlier faction fights seem peaceful. At the center of these events stood one William Morgan, a stonemason who had come to Rochester in 1822 to work on the aqueduct. During his brief stay Morgan joined the Masonic Lodge in Rochester. He moved southwest to Batavia, where he expected to use his Masonic connections to find work. He did not find a job, and the Batavia lodge refused him admittance. Rebuffed, Morgan wrote a long exposé of the secrets of Masonry and went looking for a publisher. The Rochester editor Thurlow Weed and others read his attack and would have nothing to do with it. But finally a Batavia printer took the job. Word spread that the book would be published, and Morgan came under mysterious official harassment. After a few groundless run-ins with local sheriffs, Morgan was abducted and taken to Canandaigua to face spurious charges. He was quickly released from jail—

and just as quickly kidnapped. With the help of some Rochester Masons, he was spirited through the village and imprisoned in one of the old buildings at Fort Niagara. From there he disappeared forever.[11]

Immediately, town meetings in Batavia and Canandaigua demanded an investigation, and they were joined by outraged citizens in towns throughout the region.[12] The Rochester committee, headed by Thurlow Weed and his Clintonian friends, soon gained control of an organized campaign that demanded full investigation of the kidnapping and indictments of suspected conspirators. Judges, grand jurors, and sheriffs—most of them Masons—moved slowly, and the Morgan committees began suspecting that the Masons were covering up a murder. Beginning as a citizens' investigation of one crime, the campaign widened into an attack on Masonry and its secret handshakes, secret obligations, secret ritual, and, ultimately, its secret control over society and politics.

It seems strange that men could believe Masons were plotting to take over the government of the United States. But in Rochester that was an intelligible interpretation of events. Antimasons knew the leading Masons personally. They knew the lodge included rich and powerful men, and they knew that Masons favored each other in business dealings. They knew also that Masons enjoyed the most visible signs of deference that the new community had to offer. When Rochesterians gathered to celebrate the opening of the Erie Canal in 1823, the band opened with the Masonic hymn "The Temple Is Completed."[13] Two years later, when the Marquis de Lafayette visited Rochester on his triumphant return to the United States, each of his official greeters was a Mason.[14] Suspicious and jealous non-Masons had noted all of this: "In the foundation of every public building we have beheld the interference of these mystic artisans with their symbolic insignia—in every public procession we have seen their flaunting banners, their muslin robes, and mimic crowns."[15]

But most frightening was Masonic political power. While Rochesterians petitioned the legislature for a quick investigation of Morgan's disappearance, their own representative in that body was the Mason Abelard Reynolds. James Seymour, the sheriff empowered to arrest local men implicated in the conspiracy, was another member of the lodge. There were no arrests. Probably just as well, for the judge who would have heard the cases was the Mason John Bowman. Men who were Masons held formidable political power. And under attack they used that power in secret and spiteful ways. In 1827 the Clintonian Frederick Backus was standing for his eleventh consecutive term as village treasurer. No one else had ever held the job. But in 1826 he had added his name to the Rochester Morgan committee and made powerful enemies. People assumed that Backus would again run unopposed. But when the votes were opened and counted (it was only the second time that elections were conducted by secret ballot), a write-in candidate had won. The new treasurer was John B. Elwood, a Bucktail Mason.[16]

Antimasons transformed themselves from a protest movement into a political party in 1828. With the help of his Clintonian friends, Thurlow Weed began publishing the *Anti-Masonic Enquirer* in February.[17] In March delegates from all over western New York met at Leroy and, under the direction of Weed and the Rochester committee, formed the Antimasonic Party, dedicated to preventing Masons from holding office. Of course Weed and his henchmen knew that their troubles were caused by more than Masons, and they worked to establish a connection between Masonry and the Van Buren Republicans in New York politics. It was easy. In Rochester that faction centered on Nathaniel Rochester, and the most prominent Masons were his family and friends. Grand Master of the Lodge—and the man accused of providing a carriage for Morgan's abductors—was Francis Cuming, pastor at St. Luke's Church and himself a member of the family. The colonel's son William, recently Bucktail nominee for governor, was another Mason. So were Rochester's son John and his son-in-law Jonothan Child. The Bucktail assemblyman and the slow-moving Judge Bowman, both of them old friends of the family, were also members of the lodge. John Elwood, who had become the most bitterly hated Mason in town when he sneaked into the village treasurer's post, shared a medical office with the colonel's son-in-law Anson Colman. In all, 39 percent of Bucktail leaders and only 14 percent of Clintonians were Masons.[18]

In the Antimasonic press and increasingly in the public mind, the Masonic conspiracy was linked to the Rochesters and to their Bucktail friends at Albany—friends they had used in typically "Masonic" fashion to establish the county and gain control of the bank. Clintonians had always wondered at their enemies' ability to win favors from government, and now they had a vote-winning answer:

> In the Executive of the State we have beheld a man holding the highest office in the Order, bound to his brethren by secret ties of whose nature, strength, and character we knew nothing. We have seen our legislature controlled by [Bucktail] majorities bound to the Fraternity by the same ties.[19]

Weed quickly completed the connection. Late in 1828 he accused thirteen men of using both Masonic and government funds to bribe the voters of Monroe County. Named in the handbill were nine Rochester Masons. Three of the others were Weed's rival editor, Luther Tucker, and the wealthy Democratic activists Addison Gardiner and Thomas Sheldon. The thirteenth was Martin Van Buren himself. The Masonic and Bucktail conspiracies were one and the same.[20]

Antimasonry originated in popular outrage over an unpunished murder. Thurlow Weed turned that outrage against the Van Buren Republicans in state politics and against the gen-

tlemen in Rochester who supported that faction and enjoyed
its favors. The argument between Bucktails and Clintonians
gave way to an uglier fight between Democrats and Antimasons. Much of the leadership came from the old factions, and
the controversy was in some ways continuous with the past:
Bucktails became Democrats, Clintonians became Antimasons.[21] But power within the Antimasonic and Democratic
Parties passed on to new kinds of men. Democrats included
many old Bucktails, but they were led by the combative Masons Jacob Gould and James Seymour, and by the Irish Catholic editor Henry O'Reilley. At the same time, the anti-Van
Buren forces came under the firm personal control of Thurlow Weed.

The rise of new leaders brought on a near-total collapse of
the old political families. Matthew Brown sided with the Antimasons, but he remained far from the center of power within
that movement. The Rochesters, the Strongs, and the Wards
disappeared from lists of party functionaries. To put it simply,
politics was no longer a gentleman's game. Nathaniel Rochester, for one, had been in politics all his life: as member of the
revolutionary assembly in Maryland and of the state constitu-
tional convention after the war, and as state legislator in
Maryland and New York. But while he helped govern every
community in which he lived, Rochester hated conflict. He
remembered that as a member of the Maryland legislature he
"was so disgusted with the intrigue and management among
the members, that I afterwards uniformly refused to go
again . . ."[22] In Rochester, things grew worse. The colonel
acknowledged resentment against him and agreed to sit as
president of the Bank of Rochester in 1824 only until it was
fully organized. But Thurlow Weed saw a chance to turn
jealousy of Nathaniel Rochester into votes for himself, and he
organized the People's Party largely as a public attack upon
Rochester's honesty. Under the Antimasons decorum broke
down altogether, and leaders of the old factions stepped out of

politics. Bucktails had been accused of anti-republican tendencies and of extracting undue favors from government, and
Clintonians had been labeled (in private) as a band of "scurri-
lous banditti."[23] But never before had leading citizens come
under a blanket accusation of—to name only two—treason
and murder. There was no more honor in politics.

DEMOCRACY

Antimasonry disrupted the established political elite in the
late 1820s, and it was against that backdrop that pious Rochesterians tried to discipline drifters and workingmen through
political means. In 1817 Rochester had been incorporated as a
village modeled after New England towns. Power rested with
five trustees elected annually in open town meeting. Every
man who owned property, or who worked on the roads or
served in the militia or fire department, and who had lived in
the state one year and in the county six months, could vote. In
1823 the property requirement was dropped by state law.[24]
Even these liberal requirements denied the vote to much of
Rochester's volatile population. Only 44 percent of household-
ing journeymen and laborers, for instance, stayed in Rochester
over an eight-month period in 1827.[25] No doubt frequent
moves inhibited interest in local politics among many of the
others. With voice-vote elections, and with participation limited to the more stable elements of the population, rich men
won elections. Rochester's fifty wealthiest taxpayers, along
with their relatives and business associates, accounted for 61
percent of the trustees elected between 1817 and 1825. These
men held 80 percent of the offices. Most of them, we have seen,
were the Browns and their Clintonian friends.

As trustees, they held some of the power to bring workmen
and transients under control. The charter enabled them to
collect taxes up to $1,000 and to hire a night watch and regu-
late public amusements. In 1822 they levied an annual license

fee of twenty-five dollars on ninepin alleys, shuffleboards, billiard tables, wheels of fortune, card tables, and all other gambling devices.[26] Licensing did not stop the gamblers, nor did it prevent a visitor from being robbed of $1,800 at a gambling shop in 1824.[27] The next year trustees outlawed gaming devices outright, but rather than arrest violators they collected a three-dollar monthly fine.[28] In matters of Sabbath breaking and drinking, trustees had almost no power at all. Grocers paid an annual fee of five dollars for the right to sell strong drink. Many avoided paying even that. These feeble attempts at regulation corresponded with increased offensive behavior and public disorder in the middle 1820s. The first charter had created a village government that could not control a fast-growing city. And trustees demonstrated a puzzling unwillingness to use the powers that they had. While rich men squabbled and competed for powerless and honorific positions, society was coming apart.

Inadequacies in the first charter were clear almost from the beginning, and by the middle 1820s Rochester urgently needed a new government. The village had numbered only 700 persons in 1817. It rose to 7,000 over the next nine years. There were simply too many voters for open elections. But most troublesome was the trustees' ineffectiveness in dealing with vice and disorder. Rochester petitioned the legislature for a city charter, but had to settle for a revised village charter in 1826. The second charter eliminated the most glaring inadequacies of the first. It abolished the town meeting and divided the town into five wards, each of which elected a trustee by secret ballot. More important, these trustees were empowered to "secure and enforce neatness, regularity, good order, and safety . . . and efficiently to restrain whatever may be offensive, or detrimental, to decency, good morals, or religion." Boat masters would be fined if they blew horns or bugles in the village on Sunday. Grocers could not sell liquor, serve customers, or permit gatherings of people on that day.

County officials, most of them Rochesterians, promised to scour the woods for men who spent the Lord's Day hunting and fishing. Ninepin alleys, circus riders, and theatrical representations of every kind without special license were banned.[29] "Heretofore," stated a hopeful editor, "disorder has bid defiance to wholesome law, but the presumption now is that a new state of affairs will take place."[30]

His hopes died quickly. For the new charter and the concurrent rise of Antimasonry contributed to the collapse of the old political families and to the election of new kinds of public officials. Under the first charter, trustees were elected at large and by voice vote, and one or the other of the family factions controlled the village government. To a large degree those factions were based in rivalries between land speculators. The Browns lived on their Frankfort Tract in the second ward. Nathaniel Rochester and most of his family lived in the third ward and owned much of their neighborhood. The Wards and Strongs lived on North St. Paul in the fifth ward and speculated in east-side land. With trustees elected to represent wards rather than the village at large, no faction could dominate the reorganized boards. The Brown, Ward, Strong, and Rochester family connections held nearly two-thirds of village offices between 1817 and 1825. Beginning in 1826 that figure dropped to less than one in five.[31]

More troublesome, however, was the awakening of the electorate. In 1827 the state legislature rescinded the requirement that propertyless voters work on the roads or serve in the militia or fire companies, thus adding voters who had no ties to the town's institutions.[32] And the second charter substituted general elections for the town meeting, transforming voting from a public to a private and individual act. That act was influenced not by community pressure or the stares of notables but by noise and propaganda, sometimes by violence, always by the voter's own mind. It was at this point that contests between Antimasons and Democrats penetrated elections for even the smallest offices, introducing organized party warfare into village government and contributing to the collapse of political propriety. The canvass of 1828 in particular witnessed scores of street fights. The Antimasonic editor Thurlow Weed was menaced in the streets, and the Christopher brothers rescued another Antimason from a bad beating when they pulled him into their hotel.[33] Frederick Whittlesey, the Antimasonic candidate for village clerk, was not so lucky. Confronted by an enraged Democratic blacksmith named Patrick Cavanaugh, Whittlesey stood his ground. He won the election, but went into office with a broken nose.[34] (Whittlesey, a Yale-educated lawyer and scion of one of Rochester's wealthiest families, became the Antimasons' leading streetfighter. In 1829 he was attacked and beaten again by "unknown persons," but made a comeback later that year by knocking out a prominent Democrat—in the bar at the Eagle Tavern.[35])

Election-day fighting was only the most visible sign of what had happened: village government had degenerated into politics. Members of the old officeholding elite either lost elections or quietly stepped out of politics. Under the first charter the fifty richest taxpayers and their kinsmen and associates held 80 percent of the offices; under the second they held 38 percent. At the same time the stability and continuity that town meetings and family factions had provided were lost. Between 1817 and 1825 over half the trustees were re-elected at least once. Beginning in 1826, the proportion fell to one in three.[36]

Most ominous, the new unseen electorate chose men who were unlikely to attack workingmen's controversial amusements. The following chapter will describe a campaign to enforce Sabbath observance through the use of boycotts and other kinds of force. Forty-one percent of trustees who served under the first charter affiliated with the radical Sabbatarians in 1828, while only 8 percent stood against them. Under the second charter, only 11 percent of trustees publicly favored coercive measures of enforcing Sabbath observance. A full 30 percent actively opposed them. Voters, it seems, were determined to stop pious assaults upon their freedom.

The result was that politicians dissociated themselves from Sabbatarianism and the more radical forms of temperance agitation. Antimasons in particular have been noted for their moralistic tone and for their supposed connection with Protestant churches and church-related reforms. The Democratic editor noted the same thing, and spent column after column trying to document a "holy alliance" between the Antimasons and the unpopular temperance men and Sabbatarians.[37] We shall see that he was partially correct. But leading Antimasons made it public that they had little use for religion, and even less for coercive moral reform.

Thurlow Weed, for instance, was the Antimasonic mastermind. Weed was a notorious cigar smoker and denizen of billiard rooms, and he never joined a church. In fact he mocked the most pious elements of Rochester society. In 1829 Weed ran for the assembly against Elder Jacob Gould of First Presbyterian Church. His advisors decided that he should attend services there on the Sunday before the election. He did, wearing an ill-fitting borrowed suit, "a wretched cravat, and a shocking bad hat."[38] Among the Presbyterians who witnessed this clownish performance were Elder Gould and Ashley Samson, who was president of the Monroe Sunday School Union and vice president of the New York State Temperance Society. Both Gould and Samson had taken public stands for the enforcement of the Sabbath, and both were Democrats and adamant Masons.[39] If there were members of First Church who believed that a vote for Thurlow Weed was a vote for Christ, they left services that morning with ample food for thought.

Weed's newspaper fished for votes with periodic temperance editorials (so, for that matter, did its opponent), but Antimasonic boards of trustees issued more grocery licenses at lower prices than did Democrats. And while the godly worried about the rise of vice, the *Enquirer* advertised a sure cure for gonorrhea.[40] Strangest of all, however, were Antimasonic attitudes toward the theater. That institution was a key target of militant evangelicals, but they could expect no help from Rochester's leading Antimasons. The *Enquirer* was one of the few newspapers that accepted theater advertising. Antimasonic congressman Frederick Whittlesey read his own bad poetry at the opening performance (followed by the plays "The Honeymoon" and "The Poor Soldier"), and Edwin Scrantom, publisher of the *Anti-Masonic Almanack*, enjoyed the theater as much as any man in Rochester.[41] When the theater manager was in financial trouble in 1828, Thurlow Weed and his young co-worker Henry B. Stanton organized a special performance and asked all their friends to come. The performance was a success. The manager paid his debts and stayed in business. No doubt that distressed Rochester's more pious citizens, but it gratified Thurlow Weed. He owned stock in the theater.[42]

The dissociation from churches and church-related reforms held from top to bottom within both Antimasonic and Democratic organizations. Economic and religious differences between the two parties were minimal.[43] Antimasons recruited relatively large numbers of wage earners, but Democrats were not far behind, and both parties staffed their organizations with men from every walk of life. In the churches, Democrats and Antimasons were present in almost equal numbers, although Democrats were making inroads among the humble Methodists and Catholics.[44] But the most striking aspect of the relationship between religion and politics was its weakness: only one in five activists of both parties was a full church member, and fewer than half attended services regularly. In their personal comportment, in the social makeup of their organizations, and in their campaign rhetoric, Antimasonic and Democratic politicians advertised themselves as men who had nothing to do with the gathering assault upon drinking, disorder, and irreligion.

In office, they kept their promises. After 1826 trustees could outlaw billiard rooms, the theater, neighborhood dramshops, and other workingmen's amusements. That they would refuse to use those powers became clear within the first months of the charter's operation. The trustees received an application for a theater license and quickly laid it on the table. An attempt to deny the license outright was voted down; meanwhile, the theater operated without a license. The trustees ordered the theater manager to close his doors or face prosecution. But they could not agree to enforce the order. Instead, they subjected the unruly manager to periodic fines, even when he operated on Saturday night. Apparently the theater owners found that fines could easily be deducted from their profits, and they continued to operate on that basis.[45] Even when touring companies procured the necessary license, concerned citizens protested. The *Rochester Observer* lamented that

> It is really astonishing to think that the trustees of so respectable a village as Rochester should permit such a disorderly place as the Theatre on State Street; and it is seriously to be doubted whether there is another place this side of Boanerge's regions where such a group could obtain a license from any civil authority. We express ourselves thus plainly from the knowledge that the respectable part of this community has long since decidedly disapprobated the theatre, and we do sincerely hope that our village trustees will hereafter, when an application for license is presented by any playing company, act more in accordance with the wishes of the sober, moral, and reflecting part of our citizens.[46]

It was an unhappy and increasingly clear fact, however, that the "sober and moral" part of the community no longer determined what happened in Rochester.

The same permissiveness and indecision typified actions to-

ward the groceries. After long argument the trustees decided
to raise the price of licenses rather than shut the dramshops
down. In 1827 and again in 1828 they issued nearly 100 licenses
to sell whiskey.[47] Even then, scores of grocers operated without them. When the touchy subject of unlicensed groceries
reached the trustees, Frederick Whittlesey explained that the
village lacked jurisdiction, and the board deftly and gratefully
sidestepped the question.[48] Even when grocers violated the
terms of their licenses or blatantly encouraged others to make
trouble, trustees allowed them to keep on selling drinks.
Aaron Hitchcock, for instance, operated the kind of establishment that temperance men hated most. Hitchcock owned a
small shoe shop and a house on Water Street; he took in boarders and was licensed to sell whiskey. One Sunday in 1829 he
opened his doors and allowed his neighbors to drink and make
noise. Constables descended on the house and arrested him.
He was fined five dollars and set free. His license was not
revoked.[49] Andrew Sellig, who operated a combined candy
store and dramshop on Exchange Street, was arrested in 1826
for "throwing rockets on the island." He too was fined and
permitted to keep his license.[50] Temperance men petitioned
and editorialized against the issuance of any licenses at all, but
to no avail. Rather than outlaw sin in their city, the trustees
had decided to tax it.

The reorganization of the village government, then, had
mixed effects. It gave trustees the power to outlaw sin in their
village. But at the same time secret ballot elections freed voters
from the observation of others and coincided in time with the
introduction of organized party warfare into village politics.
Regardless of their personal feelings, the candidates of both
parties were politicians first and last, and they stood before
popular majorities that invariably voted against their own
repression. Whatever the replacement for lost social controls,
it would not come from the village government.

4
Impasse

NEITHER spontaneous controls nor a faction-ridden village government could tame the workingmen and drifters who filled Rochester in the 1820s. In their own streets and neighborhoods, dissolute men did what they pleased, and anxious merchants and masters had no means of stopping them. Some rich men sensed that they had the power to coerce workmen into being good. But most were uncomfortable with power, and tried to quiet society through a moral authority that had lost its basis in everyday experience. Arguments between advocates of power and advocates of authority surfaced periodically among the village trustees. The argument widened into an open fight in 1828, as Rochester's weakened elite tried new ways of fighting social evil.

AUTHORITY: THE TEMPERANCE REFORMERS

In 1828, worried gentlemen formed the Rochester Society for the Promotion of Temperance, and affiliated with a national movement led by Lyman Beecher of Boston. These men proposed to end drunkenness through persuasion, example, and the weight of their names. Every old family and every church submerged their differences and contributed leaders to the society. Colonel Rochester himself, along with his son-in-law Jonothan Child, represented the Rochester clan and the Episcopal Church. They were joined by their old enemies Matthew Brown and Levi Ward, and by Ward's son-in-law

Moses Chapin. The Presbyterian, Baptist, and Methodist ministers were among the founders. So, temporarily, was Father McNamara of the Catholic chapel.[1] The *Observer* scanned the names and concluded that "when we see that they are the most respectable, wealthy, moral, and influential individuals in society, we feel confident that this reformation will not cease but with the extermination of intemperance from our land."[2]

The temperance reformers were wealthy men, and they possessed enormous power. But they preferred to translate power into authority, and to reform lesser men by persuasion rather than by force. Lyman Beecher, whose *Six Sermons on Intemperance* guided the movement from its beginning, defined the goal as "THE BANISHMENT OF ARDENT SPIRITS FROM THE LIST OF LAWFUL ARTICLES OF COMMERCE BY A CORRECT AND EFFICIENT PUBLIC SENTIMENT . . ." by social pressure and an aroused public opinion.[3] The society aimed its appeals at wealthy men, for these had always set standards for others. Members of the society gave up even the most moderate use of liquor. They would not buy it, drink it, sell it, manufacture it, or provide it for their guests or employees, and they would use all their influence to encourage others to do the same.[4] The organization and its methods were based on the touching faith that poor men would drink only "so long as the traffic in liquor is regarded as lawful, and is patronized by men of reputation and moral worth . . ."[5] Temperance men did not want to outlaw liquor or to run drunkards and grogsellers out of town. They wanted only to make men ashamed to drink. Reform would come quietly and voluntarily, and it would come from the top down.

Most temperance appeals were directed at businessmen and masters who hired wage labor and who were in daily contact with those elements of society with the strongest taste for alcohol. " 'I'LL LEAVE OFF WHEN THE BOSS DOES,' said a young mechanic to his companions. This shows the influence and responsibility of those who carry on an extensive business. If an employer refuses to abstain from strong drink, we need not wonder if many whom he employs refuse to abstain, encouraged by his example."[6] Temperance-minded masters stopped providing the daily dram as part of a workman's wages, and set out to convince others that work, particularly strenuous outdoor work, was better and more profitably done without the stimulus of alcohol. Master carpenters reported putting up houses "without the use of ardent spirits—*without the least difficulty.* Indeed it is much the safest way to put up frames."[7] A nearby farmer announced that he had grown tired of the "bobbling and idleness which ardent spirits uniformly produces" and that he no longer gave whiskey to his harvesters. The happy result was that "he had no difficulty in keeping them perfectly subject to his directions. They conducted and labored like sober, rational men, and not like intoxicated mutineers."[8]

Temperance propaganda promised masters social peace, a disciplined and docile labor force, and an opportunity to assert moral authority over their men. The movement enjoyed widespread success among those merchants and masters who considered themselves respectable. After one year's agitation the *Observer* announced proudly that "public opinion has already, in a great degree, branded as disgraceful, the practice of dram-drinking, among the more respectable part of the community."[9] Of course hundreds of less "respectable" men continued to drink. But temperance men stood firm in their belief that "regiments of drunkards can present but a feeble resistance compared with a few *respectable church members.*"[10]

In workshop after workshop, masters gathered their men and announced that they would no longer provide drinks or allow drinking in the shop, and that the new rules derived from patriotism and religion. Sometimes employees took a hand. When a printer's apprentice completed his training in 1829, he refused to buy his shopmates the customary round of drinks. Instead, he gave them each a Bible, a glass of cold

water, and a knowing look.[11] If a workman continued to drink
off the job, the master took him aside for a firm but friendly
talk and tried "by persuasion and all other proper and suitable
means" to bring him to his senses.[12] These must have been odd
conversations—earnest pomposity on one side, foot shuffling
and hidden grins on the other. Masters finished talking with
the assurance that they had done all that they properly could.
It only remained for workingmen to take their advice.

Underneath these gentle methods lay the assumption that
Rochester had legitimate opinion makers, and that attitudes
could radiate from them into every corner of society. Indeed
for many reformers the temperance crusade may have been a
final test of that belief. But while masters asked wage earners
to give up their evil ways, they turned workers out of their
homes and into streets and neighborhoods where drinking
remained a normal part of life. A journeyman who put up with
strange new practices on the job experienced strong pressures
to drink on his own block, where the grocery was the principal
place to relax with workmates and friends. Temperance men
talked loudest in 1828 and 1829, years in which the autonomy
of working-class neighborhoods grew at a dizzying rate. In
each of those years the village granted nearly 100 licenses to
sell whiskey by the glass, suggesting that there was a legal
drinking establishment for every twenty-eight adult men in
Rochester. These neighborhood bars dispensed nearly 200,000
gallons of whiskey annually.[13] Perhaps the workshops were
dry. The neighborhoods certainly were not.

By 1830 the temperance crusade was, on its own terms, a
success: society's leading men were encouraging abstinence.
But even as they preached, they withdrew from the social
relationships in which their ability to command obedience
was embedded. Wage earners continued to drink. But now
they drank only in their own neighborhoods and only with
each other, and in direct defiance of their employers. It taught
the masters a disheartening lesson: if authority collapsed

whenever they turned their backs, then there was in fact no authority. It was a lesson that masters were learning in a wide variety of situations. But nowhere was it dramatized more starkly than in the social relations and cultural meaning that had come to surround a glass of whiskey.

POWER: THE SABBATARIANS

The temperance movement proved once and for all that workingmen were immune to middle-class advice. From the beginning, there were men who knew that, and who suggested the use of power. Through boycotts and proscription they could force other men to give up their dissolute habits. Failing that, they could force them out of Rochester. If talk would not quiet workmen's thirst for whiskey, then godly employers should "*combine* to compel the intemperate to reform, by withholding from them any employment if they will not wholly abstain from the use of ardent spirits."[14] And if businessmen would not listen to the voice of organized morality, they could be made to experience its power. What could the godly do with merchants and distillers who resisted?

> They can, in the first place, withhold, as far as possible, the means of carrying on this nefarious and murderous business. Withhold your wood, withhold receptacles, withhold your grain, for the same reasons that you would withhold powder, pistol, and dirk from the midnight assassin. After suitable forbearance and affectionate entreaty, they can, in the second place, withhold patronage of all kinds; withdraw fellowship; treat them in all respects as felons, upon the same principle that slave dealers and incendiaries are treated as felons.[15]

These proposals flew in the face of Lyman Beecher's warning that coercion would arouse resistance and shatter the social harmony which, at bottom, temperance men were trying to create. Such ideas gained few adherents within the temperance society. But in a second effort at reform, advocates of force gained control. The result was what Beecher had predicted: failure, and an open and debilitating fight between society's leading men.

Among the problems that came to Rochester with the Erie Canal, none but intemperance was more troublesome than violation of the Sabbath. Rochester businessmen and masters had been born into villages where it was a punishable offense to cook after sundown on Saturday or to leave the house during the next twenty-four hours for any purpose other than going to church. This was true not only in the countryside but in the largest towns. Passing through in 1831, Tocqueville marveled that "Boston on Sunday has, literally, the appearance of a deserted town."[16] Rochester, however, was a different kind of city. Freight and passenger boats operated seven days a week, and activity along the canal and on the loading docks went unabated on the Lord's Day. Rochester's concerned citizens were helpless. When the Reverend Joseph Penney of First Presbyterian Church petitioned the state legislature to shut down the locks on Sunday the lawmakers refused, and asked Penney if he really wanted hundreds of boatmen and transients stranded in his village on Sundays. Some of Penney's wealthiest neighbors agreed: not only was six-day travel bad for business, but boatmen would use their free Sundays to "drink grog and court Venus."[17]

With Sabbath breakers, the state government, and businessmen in their own town ignoring them, Rochester Sabbatarians held one more weapon: they could force boat owners to stop doing business on Sunday. In 1828 they began pressuring the forwarding merchants. One small line had already stopped Sunday travel, and the first public meeting of Sabbatarians announced that "we will give our business and patronage to such lines as do not travel on the Holy Sabbath," something very much like a boycott of the other lines.[18] Sabbatarians demanded that people abstain from Sunday travel and that they deny patronage to the seven-day lines even on weekdays. They knew that workingmen and transients would not reform voluntarily, and their stated aim was *"to act on the owners of steamboats, stages, canal boats, and livery stables; and through the medium of their pockets, to prevent them from furnishing conveyances on the Sabbath, for that large mass of the community who neither fear God nor obey man."*[19]

Almost simultaneously, Elder Josiah Bissell of Third Presbyterian Church, with donations from rich townsmen and from such pious outsiders as Lewis Tappan of New York, organized a Sabbath-keeping stage and boat line. The Pioneer Line, as the venture was called, did not operate on Sunday. The boats and coaches did not run, tickets were not sold, horses were not shod, boats were not repaired. The stage drivers and boatmen were non-drinkers, and at stops the Pioneer stages served hot coffee rather than the customary rum. The Rochester House and Christopher's Mansion House closed their bars and affiliated with the Pioneer, offering safe, suitable accommodations to travelers on the Pioneer Line.[20] When businessmen argued that the end of Sunday travel would impair delivery of the mail, Elder Bissell went to Washington to secure post-office contracts for the Pioneer. Rebuffed, he returned to Rochester and, in concert with Lewis Tappan and Lyman Beecher, organized a nationwide campaign to abolish transportation of the mail and the opening of post offices on Sunday. Overnight, Rochester was at the center of a national crusade to maintain Sunday as sacred time.[21]

Pioneer tactics were alien to the spirit of the gentler reformers: Bissell and his friends called for boycotts of non-cooperating businessmen. Immediately they found themselves opposed by some of the richest and most pious men in Rochester. These claimed to be as disturbed as anyone else by violations of the eighth commandment. But they felt that compulsion and boycotts were "contrary to the free spirit of our institutions." Pioneer tactics were a threat to individual conscience, and these gentlemen "resolved, unanimously, that we invite all good men to aid us in promoting, temperately, but with firmness, the great interests of morality and social order; blending the humility and meekness of the Christian with the benevolence of the philanthropist."[22] Boycotts in particular aroused a shocked and angry opposition. The *Observer*, staunch supporter of the Pioneers, admitted that a lot of good Christians were repulsed:

> They consider them as wrong in principle, contrary to the spirit of the Gospel, and inconsistent with that universal tolera-tion of religious opinions, which is allowed by the laws of our country. They contend, that all combinations of Christians to withdraw their business and patronage from any class of men, on account of their belief and practice in matters of religion, is a sort of compulsion and an invasion of the rights of conscience, which is inconsistent with the law of kindness to our neighbor and an injury to the cause of the Redeemer.[23]

Early in 1829 word came that the Sabbath mails petitions had been rejected. Senator Richard Johnson, to whose Post Office Committee the memorials had been referred, explained that the federal government could not make laws concerning reli-gion, and that in any event the new economy demanded a seven-day circulation of information. Johnson urged Sab-batarians to give up their new political course and suggested that they return to the old and ineffective methods of gentle persuasion: "Would it not be more congenial to the prospects of Christians," he asked, "to appeal exclusively to the great Law-giver of the universe to aid them in making men better, in correcting their practices by purifying their hearts?"[24] Johnson's *Report* was the classic Jacksonian statement on rela-tions between church and state. It was also a shrewd and powerful political tract, and it helped win Johnson the Vice Presidency of the United States in 1836. In Rochester, Sab-batarians were surprised and dismayed. But a Quaker publisher who had stood against them printed thousands of copies of the *Report*, some of them bound in white satin, and advertised them as "a supplement to our Bill of Rights."[25]

The Pioneers rejected moral authority as a means of reforming society. They did not care if dissolute men wanted to break the Sabbath. They wanted only to make them stop doing it. The result was a sharp religious and moral division within the elite. Both Sabbatarians and the men who opposed them were rich and respectable. But fully two-thirds of the Sabbatarians were Presbyterians, and their Sabbath mails petition included the signatures of three clergymen of that denomination and, in sharp contrast to the temperance society, none from other churches.[26] Throughout the career of the Pioneer Line, the *Observer* denied charges that the movement was dominated by Presbyterians, but those charges had solid roots in fact.[27]

More than half the anti-Sabbatarians were non-church members, but their leadership included some of Rochester's leading Protestant laymen. The Quaker Elihu Marshall lent his voice and the voice of his newspaper to the struggle of conscience against compulsion. Heman Norton, recently elected to the assembly as an Antimason, was one of the forwarding merchants under attack, and he too fought the Pioneers—from within First Presbyterian Church. Jonothan Child, whose Pilot Line was the largest fleet of packets on the canal, led a large Rochester family contingent into the fight. Child had few doubts about his own sense of responsibility. He was, like Marshall and Norton, an ardent temperance man. He was also vestryman at St. Luke's Church, and he maintained a strict moral police over his boat crews. But neither Child nor his wealthy friends liked being coerced. The Sabbatarians read the list of men who opposed them and shook their heads. "There may be something imposing," stated the *Observer*,

in the respectability of some of the names connected with these
singular proceedings, but the Christian will reflect that
the "great, mighty, and noble," or the wise men of this world,
are not always the humble followers of our Savior and may
not be the safest guides in things of a moral and religious
nature . . .[28]

Rich Christians were fighting in public.

By 1829 the Pioneer Line was a failure and a national laugh-
ingstock. But during its noisy and ineffectual career the Sabbatarian crusade split Rochester's ruling elite and wakened
humbler men to the dangers of religious control. In the streets
and on the canal, opposition to the Pioneer Line was immediate and sometimes violent. Pioneer handbills were torn down
as fast as they could be put up, and strangers asking the way
to the Pioneer offices were given bad directions. Rival boat
crews made life miserable for men on the Pioneer packets. On
one journey a Sabbath-keeping boat tried to pass one of the
larger and slower freight boats. Men on the seven-day boat
dumped two horses into the canal, cut in at locks, tore planks
from the towpath to foul the Pioneer horses, cast loose a water-
logged barge to obstruct passage of the faster boat, and cut the
Pioneer tow rope three times.[29] As we have seen, opposition
took quieter and more effective forms at the polls. Men who
supported the Pioneers and made their support public almost
invariably lost elections in the late 1820s. Elisha Johnson, a
wealthy Democrat who was active in the anti-Sabbatarian organization, won election to three consecutive terms as village
president between 1827 and 1829.

The Pioneers had sought to mobilize the power of wealthy
men and turn it to the task of policing others. Instead, they
split the elite and gave workingmen a clear idea of who their
enemies were.

CHURCHES AND POLITICS IN 1830

Battles over politics and reform in the late 1820s splintered the elite and left combatants bruised and angry. Sabbatarians advertised the perversity and religious ignorance of even their most pious opponents, and Antimasonry was based on the contention that every Mason was accomplice to murder. Public life lost its last traces of civility. For all their feuding and pouting, Bucktails and Clintonians had worked together whenever the interests of the business community as a whole were at stake: in lobbying for the county and for the bank charter and—for the last time—in forming the temperance society. Now political contests degenerated into vicious public fights followed by lawsuits and personal grudges that dragged on for years.[30] It was a hopelessly divided elite that met the social crisis of the late 1820s.

Public life in Rochester had become an incoherent and many-sided squabble. But underneath the confusion there were two roughly continuous leadership factions throughout the late 1820s. One united Antimasons, Sabbatarians, and—to a lesser degree—temperance advocates. The other linked Democrats, Masons, and anti-Sabbatarians.[31] Thus political groupings corresponded to the argument over means. The first faction included most advocates of force. The second included opponents of force and/or men who had experienced coercion at first hand. When the remaining Masons—almost all of them Democrats—tried to end the controversy by dissolving the lodge in 1829, they betrayed the now-familiar hurt feelings of gentlemen under attack:

> Our appeal is to the friends of Peace and Good Order; and if the waters of strife are to be poured out, without reserve, embittering all the relations of life—if an unrelenting crusade is to be carried on against a numerous and respectable portion of our fellow men, merely on account of their speculative opinions, *the responsibility will not rest upon us!*[32]

Antimasons, Sabbatarians, and a minority within the temperance movement were discovering the uses of power. Their opponents recoiled at methods that forced Masons to give up their charters and excluded them from some churches, that denied employment and patronage to men who continued to drink or to belong to the Masonic Lodge, and that coerced businessmen into supporting the Sabbath measures.[33] Few of these men, whatever their political positions, looked with approval upon public drunkenness, Sabbath breaking, or the murder of William Morgan. But there was an impassable line between advocates of force and advocates of gentler means, and it split Rochester's elite into angry halves.

Unhappily, the argument spilled beyond politics, disrupting families and friendships, and dividing every Protestant church in town. Politics in the early 1820s had followed family lines. A by-product was relative unanimity within churches. Nathaniel Rochester could look back from his pew at St. Luke's and nod to a house full of kinsmen and allies. Across the street at First Presbyterian, the Browns and Wards could do the same. Thus political divisions strengthened the sense of unity and common purpose within communities of believers. Late in the decade, however, the dividing line in politics was not kinship but ideology. Political fights were violent and personal, and they took place within Protestant congregations as well as between them. True, Antimasons and—especially—Sabbatarians tended to be Presbyterians. But with the withdrawal of the Rochesters and their Episcopalian allies, opposition to Antimasons fell more and more to Masons who were Presbyterians, and the correlation between political groups and denominations broke down.[34] Leaders on both sides were present in nearly every church, and some of the ugliest disputes took place within the town's troubled congregations.

St. Luke's, for instance, was the old headquarters of the Rochesters and their Bucktail friends. It was here that anti-Sabbatarians found their most respectable supporters, and it was here that many prominent Masons spent Sunday mornings. The pastor was Francis Cuming, one of the Rochester in-laws. The Reverend Cuming was also the highest-ranking Mason in Rochester, having been installed as Grand Commander in 1826—in ceremonies held at St. Luke's Church.[35] Cuming was among the first to speak in defense of the lodge, and Antimasons accused him of helping with the kidnapping and eventually had him indicted. Cuming reacted bitterly, and preached from his pulpit against the Antimasons. No doubt most of the congregation sympathized. But there were men at St. Luke's who had helped to bring on the minister's troubles. Timothy Childs, the first Antimason sent to Congress, heard Cuming's counterattacks on his party. So did Thurlow Weed's henchman Frederick Whittlesey, who had been elected vestryman at St. Luke's a few months before Morgan's disappearance. Men who hated each other shared the pews, and St. Luke's became an uncomfortable place in which to worship. At the center of the controversy, Francis Cuming came under terrible pressure, both from outside and from within his church. In 1829 he resigned and left Rochester.[36]

Across the river, the crossfire of the late 1820s created another unpleasant situation at St. Paul's Church, which had been organized in 1827 as the second Episcopal congregation. The two leading members were Elisha Johnson and William Atkinson. Johnson was an adamant anti-Sabbatarian. Atkinson was one of Josiah Bissell's partners on the Pioneer Line and, to confound every pattern, one of the few Masons who continued to defend the lodge as late as 1829. When it came time to call a minister, the vestry invited Charles McIlvaine, a Low Churchman. Immediately the west-side Episcopalians, led by Thomas Hart Rochester and Jonothan Child, objected. With their support the Rev. H. U. Onderdonck of Brooklyn warned the people at St. Paul's that McIlvaine was a graduate of Princeton Seminary, a dedicated evangelical, and "a zealous promoter of the schemes that would blend us with Presbyteri-

ans."[37] That seems to have been what the Sabbatarian William
Atkinson wanted, and he led the vestry into an ugly battle
with the meddlers at St. Luke's. The Rochester family won,
and St. Paul's withdrew the invitation to McIlvaine and
adopted High Church ritual in 1829.[38] But not before leading
Episcopalians had taken turns insulting each other in public.

There were even nastier disputes between Presbyterians.
Here the fighting centered on one man: Elder Josiah Bissell of
Third Church. Bissell was a crusader. He had headed the
Monroe County Bible Society (the first in the nation to devise
the plan of giving free Bibles to the poor) since its founding,
and he financed the militant *Rochester Observer* from his own
pocket. A member of the original Morgan committee, Bissell
was founder and operator of the Pioneer Line. He was also a
remarkably abrasive and self-righteous man. Lyman Beecher,
who worked with Bissell on the Sabbath mails campaign, complained that "our good brother Bissell may need some caution" in his dealings with wealthy but moderate benefactors,
and indeed Bissell's demands for donations paid little attention to the feelings of philanthropists.[39]

Josiah Bissell's zeal had caused sporadic fights within his
denomination throughout the 1820s. He became the center of
continuous controversy in 1828, when his Pioneer Line and
his Sabbath mails campaign made him the personification of
proscriptive and coercive measures. One weekday Bissell spot-
ted the Rev. William James of Second Church riding one of the
seven-day stages. He intervened at Second Church and in-
formed James that his congregation no longer wanted him.
Joseph Penney of First Church entered the dispute on the side
of his fellow minister and publicized intradenominational hos-
tilities that had been brewing for years.

> I regard Elder Bissell as an active man, prosecuting everything
> he does with untiring zeal and energy. But there is no distinc-
> tion with him in his beneficial or injurious purposes, all are the

same if he has enlisted in them; they are pursued with the same
spirit, right or wrong . . . I do not impute his measures to
wicked motives; but to a willful course, deprecated by many,
lamented by all, and perverting the influence of the church.[40]

Bissell's plan, evidently, was to remove such moderates as
Penney and James and replace them with militant evangelicals
with whom he could work more closely. But the plan only
aroused a bitter and demoralizing fight within all three congregations, each of which included large numbers of Bissell's
friends and enemies. Like the Episcopalians, Presbyterians
could not worship without enemies at their sides.

By the end of the decade, churchgoing businessmen and
masters had lost faith in their ability to govern. Beneath them
was a new and unruly and altogether necessary urban working
class. Masters had always governed such men spontaneously,
in face-to-face transactions that were a part of everyday routine. That system collapsed in the middle and late 1820s. Now
attempts to influence the actions of workingmen through authority and persuasion were unsuccessful and—worse—humil-
iating. Village officials, elected by the majority that many
wished to regulate, did nothing. In 1828 some militant Christian businessmen tried to reestablish control through force.
They failed, and in the course of failing they split the churchgoing community into warring camps. By 1830 the temperance and Sabbatarian crusades were bankrupt and ready to
dissolve, and mystified church members fought each other
until they were numb. The life went out of Rochester Protestantism. After steady gains throughout the 1820s and a hopeful
revival in 1827, conversions stopped. In every church, the
number of new members dropped dramatically in 1828 and
1829 and through the fall of 1830.[41]

Late in 1829 Elder Josiah Bissell wrote the evangelist
Charles Finney. Bissell's attempt to christianize the post office
was the butt of jokes. His six-day transport line drained his

fortune and then failed, and at least half the Protestant church members in Rochester hated him personally. (There was trouble even at home. Bissell's father, a merchant in Pittsfield, Massachusetts, had fought drunkenness by taking liquor off his shelves. But he insisted that it was both "impolitic and improper . . . to enter into any combination for the coercive regulation of . . . opinions or habits."[42]) Bissell told Finney of his problems with Penney and James, and described a few "specimens of the large budget of evils rolling through our land & among us," dwelling on the moral dangers of canal life. He confessed that the good people of Rochester felt powerless to do anything about it: "the people & the church say it cannot be helped—and why do they say this? Because the state of religion is so low; because they know not the power of the Gospel of Jesus. 'Through Christ Jesus strengthening us we can do all things,' and if so it is time we were about it."[43]

5
Pentecost

CHARLES GRANDISON FINNEY came to Rochester in September 1830. For six months he preached in Presbyterian churches nearly every night and three times on Sunday, and his audience included members of every sect. During the day he prayed with individuals and led an almost continuous series of prayer meetings. Soon there were simultaneous meetings in churches and homes throughout the village. Pious women went door-to-door praying for troubled souls. The high school stopped classes and prayed. Businessmen closed their doors early and prayed with their families. "You could not go upon the streets," recalled one convert, "and hear any conversation, except upon religion."[1] By early spring the churches faced the world with a militance and unity that had been unthinkable only months before, and with a boundless and urgent sense of their ability to change society. In the words of its closest student, ". . . no more impressive revival has occurred in American history."[2]

NEW MEASURES

First, a word on the evangelical plan of salvation. Man is innately evil and can overcome his corrupt nature only through faith in Christ the redeemer—that much is common to Christianity in all its forms. Institutional and theological differences among Christians trace ultimately to varying means of attaining that faith. The Reformation abolished sa-

cred beings, places, and institutions that had eased the path
between the natural and supernatural worlds. Without ritual,
without priest-magicians, without divine immanence in an
institutional church, Protestants face God across infinite
lonely space. They bridge that space through prayer—through
the state of absolute selflessness and submission known generally as transcendence. The experience of transcending oneself
and this world through prayer is for Protestants direct experience of the Holy Ghost, and it constitutes assurance of salvation, sanctification, and new life.

Prayer, then, is the one means by which a Protestant estab-
lishes his relation with God and his assurance that he is one
of God's people. Prayer is a personal relationship between
God and man, and the decision whether that relationship is
established belongs to God. No Protestants dispute that. But
they have argued endlessly on man's ability to influence the
decision. The evangelical position was phrased (and it was
understood by its detractors) as an increase in human ability
so great that prayer and individual salvation were ultimately
voluntary. Hurried notes to Charles Finney's Rochester sermons insisted: "It should in all cases be required now to repent, now to give themselves up to God, now to say and feel
Lord here I am take me, it's all I can do. And when the sinner
can do that . . . his conversion is attained."[3] "The truth,"
he explained, "is employed to influence men, prayer to move
God . . . I do not mean that God's mind is changed by prayer . . . But prayer produces such a change *in us* as renders it
consistent for him to do otherwise."[4] To hyper-Calvinists who
protested that this filled helpless man with false confidence,
Finney shouted, "What is that but telling them to hold on to
their rebellion against God? . . . as though God was to blame
for not converting them."[5] The only thing preventing individual conversion was the individual himself.

This reevaluation of human ability caught the evangelicals
in a dilemma. But it was a dilemma they had already solved in

practice. Finney and his friends insisted that God granted new life in answer to faithful prayer. But the ability to pray with faith was itself experimental proof of conversion. By definition, the unregenerate could not pray. For Finney there was a clear and obvious way out, a way that he and Rochester Protestants witnessed hundreds of times during the revival winter: "Nothing is more calculated to beget a spirit of prayer, than to unite in social prayer with one who has the spirit himself."[6] That simple mechanism is at the heart of evangelical Protestantism.

Conversion had always ended in prayer and humiliation before God. But ministers had explained the terms of salvation and left terrified sinners to wrestle with it alone. Prayer was transacted in private between a man and his God, and most middle-class Protestants were uncomfortable with public displays of humiliation. As late as 1829, Rochester Presbyterians had scandalized the village when they began to kneel rather than stand at prayer.[7] More than their theological implications, Finney's revival techniques aroused controversy because they transformed conversion from a private to a public and intensely social event. The door-to-door canvass, the intensification of family devotions, prayer meetings that lasted till dawn, the open humiliation of sinners on the anxious bench: all of these transformed prayer and conversion from private communion into spectacular public events.

What gave these events their peculiar force was the immediatist corollary to voluntary conversion. The Reverend Whitehouse of St. Luke's Church (yes, the Episcopalians too) explained it in quiet terms:

> Appeals are addressed to the heart and the appeals are in reference to the present time. And each time the unconverted sinner leaves the house of God without having closed with the terms of the Gospel he rejects the offer of mercy. Had some future time been specified as that in which we were to make a decision

we might listen time after time to the invitations and reject them. But it is expressly said today and now is the accepted time.[8]

Initially, these pressures fell on the already converted. It was the prayers of Christians that led others to Christ, and it was their failure to pray that sent untold millions into hell. Lay evangelicals seldom explained the terms of salvation in the language of a Reverend Whitehouse—or even of a Charles Finney. But with the fate of their children and neighbors at stake, they carried their awful responsibility to the point of emotional terrorism. Finney tells the story of a woman who prayed while her son-in-law attended an anxious meeting. He came home converted, and she thanked God and fell dead on the spot.[9] Everard Peck reported the death of his wife to an unregenerate father-in-law, and told the old man that his dead daughter's last wish was to see him converted.[10] "We are either marching towards heaven or towards hell," wrote one convert to his sister. "How is it with you?"[11]

The new measures brought sinners into intense and public contact with praying Christians. Conversion hinged not on private prayer, arbitrary grace, or intellectual choice, but on purposive encounters between people. The secret of the Rochester revival and of the attendant transformation of society lay ultimately in the strategy of those encounters.

While Finney led morning prayer meetings, pious women visited families. Reputedly they went door-to-door. But the visits were far from random. Visitors paid special attention to the homes of sinners who had Christian wives, and they arrived in the morning hours when husbands were at work. Finney himself found time to pray with Melania Smith, wife of a young physician. The doctor was anxious for his soul, but sickness in the village kept him busy and he was both unable to pray and unwilling to try. But his wife prayed and tormented him constantly, reminding him of "the woe which is denounced against the families which call not on the Name of the Lord."[12] Soon his pride broke and he joined her as a member of Brick Presbyterian Church. Finney's wife, Lydia, made a bolder intrusion into the home of James Buchan, a merchant-tailor and a Roman Catholic whose wife, Caroline, was a Presbyterian. Buchan, with what must have been enormous self-restraint, apologized for having been out of the house, thanked Finney for the tract, and invited him and his wife to tea.[13] (It is not known whether Finney accepted the invitation, but this was one bit of family meddling which may have backfired. In 1833 Caroline Buchan withdrew from the Presbyterian Church and converted to Catholicism.) In hundreds of cases the strategy of family visits worked. As the first converts fell, the *Observer* announced with satisfaction that the largest group among them was "young heads of families."[14]

Revival enthusiasm began with the rededication of church members and spread to the people closest to them. Inevitably, much of it flowed through family channels. Finney claimed Samuel D. Porter, for instance, as a personal conquest. But clearly he had help. Porter was an infidel, but his sister in Connecticut and his brother-in-law Everard Peck were committed evangelicals. Porter came under a barrage of family exhortation, and in January Peck wrote home that "Samuel is indulging a trembling hope . . ." He remained the object of family prayer for eight more months before hope turned into assurance. Then he joined his sister and brother-in-law in praying for the soul of their freethinking father.[15] The realtor Bradford King left another record of evangelism within and between related households. After weeks of social prayer and private agony, he awoke and heard himself singing, *"I am going to the Kingdom will you come along with me."* He testified at meeting the next day, but did not gain assurance until he returned home and for the first time prayed with his family. He rose and "decided that as for me & my house we would serve the Lord." Immediately King turned newfound powers

on his brother's house in nearby Bloomfield. After two months
of visiting and prayer he announced, "We had a little pentecost at brothers . . . all were praising and glorifying God in one
United Voice."[16] The revival made an evangelist of every convert, and most turned their power on family members.

Charles Finney's revival was based on group prayer. It was
a simple, urgent activity that created new hearts in hundreds
of men and women, and it generated—indeed it relied upon—
a sense of absolute trust and common purpose among participants. The strengthening of family ties that attended the revival cannot be overestimated. But it was in prayer meetings
and evening services that evangelism spilled outside old social
channels, laying the basis for a transformed and united Protestant community.

Bradford King had no patience for "Old Church Hipocrites
who think more of their particular denomination than Christ
Church,"[17] and his sentiments were rooted in an astonishing
resolution of old difficulties. Presbyterians stopped fighting during the first few days, and peace soon extended to the
other denominations. Before the first month was out, Finney
marveled that "Christians of every denomination generally
seemed to make common cause, and went to work with a will,
to pull sinners out of the fire."[18] The most unexpected portent
came in October, when the weight of a crowded gallery spread
the walls and damaged the building at First Church. Vestrymen at St. Paul's—most of them former Masons and bitter
enemies of the Presbyterians—let that homeless congregation
into their church.[19] But it was in prayer meetings and formal
services that the collective regeneration of a fragmented
churchgoing community took place, for it was there that
"Christians of different denominations are seen mingled together in the sanctuary on the Sabbath, and bowing at the
same altar in the social prayer meeting."[20]

Crowded prayer meetings were held almost every night
from September until early March, and each of them was

managed carefully. When everyone was seated the leader read a short verse dealing with the object of prayer. Satisfied that everyone understood and could participate, he called on those closest to the spirit. These prayed aloud, and within minutes all worldly thoughts were chased from the room. (Finney knew that the chemistry of prayer worked only when everyone shared in it, and he discouraged attendance by scoffers, cranks, and the merely curious.) Soon sinners grew anxious; some of them broke into tears, and Christians came close to pray with them. Then followed the emotional displays that timid ministers had feared, but which they accepted without a whimper during the revival winter. In October Artemissia Perkins prayed with her fiancé in Brick Church. Suddenly her voice rose above the others, and over and over she prayed, "Blessed be the Name of Jesus," while her future husband, her neighbors, and people who never again could be strangers watched and participated in the awesome work.[21] It was in hundreds of encounters such as this that the revival shattered old divisions and laid the foundation for moral community among persons who had been strangers or enemies. "I know this is all algebra to those who have never felt it," Finney explained. "But to those who have experienced the agony of wrestling, prevailing prayer, for the conversion of a soul, you may depend on it, that soul . . . appears as dear as a child is to the mother who brought it forth with pain."[22]

At formal services this mechanism took on massive proportions.[23] During services Christians gathered in other churches and nearby homes to pray for the evangelist's success. Sometimes crowds of people who could not find seats in the house prayed outside in the snow. Downstairs the session room was packed, and every break in the lecture was punctuated by the rise and fall of prayer.

Inside, every seat was filled. People knelt in the aisles and doorways. Finney reserved seats near the pulpit for anxious sinners—not random volunteers, but prominent citizens who had spoken with him privately. None sat on the anxious bench who was not almost certain to fall. Separated from the regenerate and from hardened sinners, their conversions became grand public spectacles. In the pulpit, Finney preached with enormous power, but with none of the excesses some people expected. He had dropped a promising legal career to enter the ministry, and his preaching demonstrated formidable courtroom skills, not cheap theatrics. True, he took examples from everyday experience and spoke in folksy, colloquial terms. (With what may have been characteristic modesty, he reminded his listeners that Jesus had done the same.) Most of his lectures lasted an hour, but it was not uncommon for a packed church to listen twice that long "without the movement of a foot." When he gestured at the room, people ducked as if he were throwing things. In describing the fall of sinners he pointed to the ceiling, and as he let his finger drop people in the rear seats stood to watch the final entry into hell. Finney spoke directly to the anxious bench in front of him, and at the close of the lecture he demanded immediate repentance and prayer. Some of Rochester's first citizens humbled themselves on the anxious bench, sweating their way into heaven surrounded by praying neighbors. It was the most spectacular of the evangelist's techniques, and the most unabashedly communal.

NEW CHRISTIANS

Charles Finney's revival created a community of militant evangelicals that would remake society and politics in Rochester. The work of that community will fill the remainder of this book. But now it is time to keep promises made in the Introduction, to attempt a systematic explanation of Finney's triumph at Rochester. The pages that follow isolate the individuals who joined churches while Finney was in town, then locate experiences that they shared and that explain why they and not others were ripe for conversion in 1830–31. Insofar as the revival can be traced to its social origins, I shall consider it traceable to those experiences.

Finney claimed to have converted "the great mass of the most influential people" in Rochester.[24] The *Observer* agreed that new church members included most of the town's "men of wealth, talents, and influence—those who move in the highest circles of society,"[25] and church records reinforce those claims. Table 3 compares the occupational status of Finney's male converts with that of men who joined churches in the years 1825–29. (Pre-revival figures are limited to the four years surrounding the tax list of 1827. Occupations of Finney converts are derived from the 1830 assessment rolls. Thus each occupation in the table is measured within two years of the time of conversion.)

TABLE 3. OCCUPATIONS OF THE NEW MALE ADMITTANTS TO ROCHESTER PROTESTANT CHURCHES IN THE LATE 1820s, AND IN THE REVIVAL OF 1830–31 (PERCENTAGES)

	year of admission	
	1825–29 (N=85)	1830–31 (N=170)
businessman-professional	22	19
shopkeeper-petty proprietor	14	11
master craftsman	16	26
clerical employee	12	10
journeyman craftsman	24	22
laborer-semiskilled	13	12

NOTE: The 1825–29 figures are derived from the tax list and directory of 1827. Figures for the years 1830–31 are derived from the 1830 tax list and the directories of 1827 and/or 1834. To ensure that these men were in Rochester when the tax list was compiled, inclusion is limited to those who appear in the 1827 directory or the 1830 census.

Both in the 1820s and in the revival of 1830–31, new church members came disproportionately from among businessmen, professionals, and master workmen. During the Finney revival conversions multiplied dramatically within every group. But the center of enthusiasm shifted from the stores and offices to the workshops. Indeed it is the sharp increase in conversions among master craftsmen that accounts for slight declines in every other group. Whatever the problems that prepared the ground for Finney's triumph, they were experienced most strongly by master workmen.

TABLE 4. PERCENT PROTESTANT CHURCH MEMBERS AMONG SELECTED PROPRIETORS, 1827–34

	1827	1834	percent change
merchant (N=73, 63)	23	33	+30
hotelkeeper (N=14, 30)*	21	13	−38
doctor (N=21, 28)	29	54	+46
lawyer (N=23, 31)	22	58	+62
grocer (N=80, 59)	9	31	+71
forwarding merchant (N=7, 18)	14	50	+72
master builder (N=14, 13)†	21	69	+70
master shoemaker (N=15, 15)†	20	73	+73
small-shop proprietor (N=20, 37)†	30	62	+52

*Includes tavernkeepers and innkeepers.
†Includes only those identified as masters through newspaper advertisements and antiquarian sources.

Table 4 begins the attempt to infer just what those problems were. The table isolates specific occupations within the business community and calculates the percentage of church members within them in 1827 and again in 1834. Increases were most spectacular among master craftsmen and manufacturers, but there were significant variations within that group. Master builders and shoemakers had made dramatic breaks with the traditional organization of work, and with customary relations between masters and journeymen. The proportions of church members among them increased 70 percent and 73 percent, respectively. Proprietors of the small indoor workshops participated in the revival, but their increase was a less impressive 51 percent. Change in the operations they controlled came more slowly. They hired relatively few journeymen, and they continued into the 1830s to incorporate many of those men into their homes.

Among white-collar proprietors, lawyers, forwarding merchants, and grocers made the greatest gains: 62 percent, 72 percent, and 71 percent, respectively. Rochester was the principal shipping point on the Erie Canal, and most boats operating on the canal belonged to Rochester forwarders. It was their boat crews who were reputedly the rowdiest men in an unruly society, and it was the forwarders who had been the chief target of the Sabbatarian crusade. Grocers were another white-collar group with peculiarly close ties to the working class. The principal retailers of liquor, they were closely regulated by the village trustees. In 1832 the trustees not only doubled the price of grocery licenses but began looking into the moral qualifications of applicants.[26] The increased religiosity among grocers (as well as the decline in the total number of men in that occupation) reflects that fact. Reformers had branded forwarders and grocers the supporters both of the most dangerous men in society and of their most dangerous habits. While they had resisted attacks on their livelihood, grocers and boat owners could not but agree to their complicity in the collapse of old social forms. Most of them remained outside the churches. But a startlingly increased minority joined with master workmen and cast their lots with Jesus.

With these occupations removed, the revival among white-collar proprietors was weak. Doctors and merchants had only tenuous links with the new working class, and little personal responsibility for the collapse of the late 1820s. Increases among them were 46 percent and 30 percent, respectively. Hotelkeepers in particular were divorced from contact with workingmen, for they were dependent for their livelihoods on the more well-to-do canal travelers. Church membership among hotelkeepers actually declined 38 percent during the revival years. (The one remaining occupation—the law—was a special case: the increase was 62 percent. No doubt part of the explanation lies in Finney himself, who was a former attorney and took special pride in the conversion of lawyers. But perhaps more important is the fact that many lawyers were politicians, and in the 1830s resistance to the churches was political suicide.)

With few exceptions, then, Charles Finney's revival was strongest among entrepreneurs who bore direct responsibility for disordered relations between classes. And they were indeed responsible. The problem of social class arose in towns and cities all over the northern United States after 1820. It would be easy to dismiss it as a stage of urban-industrial growth, a product of forces that were impersonal and inevitable. In some ways it was. But at the beginning the new relationship between master and wage earner was created by masters who preferred money and privacy to the company of their workmen and the performance of old patriarchal duties. Available evidence suggests that it was precisely those masters who filled Finney's meetings.

TABLE 5. COMPOSITION OF HOUSEHOLDS HEADED BY PROPRIETORS IN 1827, BY RELIGIOUS STATUS OF HOUSEHOLDERS

| householder | N | percent which included | | |
		kin	boarders	employees
church member in 1829	81	15	14	41
revival convert	89	8	7	33
non-church member	151	13	17	43

Perhaps more than any other act, the removal of workmen from the homes of employers created an autonomous working class. Table 5 compares households headed in 1827 by proprietors who joined churches during the revival with those headed by non-church members and by men who belonged to

churches before the revival. Finney's converts kept fewer
workmen in their families than did other proprietors, suggesting either that they had removed many of those men or that
they had never allowed them into their homes. Table 6 traces
households that included "extra" adult men in 1827 over the
next three years. The table is compiled from the 1830 census.
That document names heads of households and identifies others by age and sex. By counting males over the age of sixteen
(the age at which men were included in the 1827 directory, and
thus in Table 5), we may trace the broadest outlines of household change in the years immediately preceding the revival.
Most proprietors thinned their families between 1827 and
1830. But while old church members and those who stayed
outside the churches removed one in four adult men, converts
cut their number by more than half.[27] Thus the analyses of
occupations and of household structure point clearly to one
conclusion: Finney's converts were entrepreneurs who had
made more than their share of the choices that created a free-
labor economy and a class-bounded society in Rochester.

TABLE 6. CHANGES IN THE COMPOSITION OF HOUSEHOLDS HEADED BY
PROPRIETORS, 1827–30, BY RELIGIOUS STATUS OF HOUSEHOLDERS

householder*	number of males over 16 years		
	1827	1830	percent change
church member in 1829	67	48	−24
revival convert	74	31	−58
non-church member	113	80	−29

*Includes only householders who appear in both the 1827 directory and the
1830 census.

The transformation began in the workshops, but it was not
contained there. For in removing workmen the converts altered their own positions within families. The relative absence
of even boarders and distant kin in their homes suggests a
concern with domestic privacy. And within those families

housewives assumed new kinds of moral authority. The organization of prayer meetings, the pattern of family visits, and
bits of evidence from church records suggest that hundreds of
conversions culminated when husbands prayed with their
wives. Women formed majorities of the membership of every
church at every point in time. But in every church, men increased their proportion of the communicants during revivals,
indicating that revivals were family experiences and that
women were converting their men.[28] In 1830–31 fully 65 percent of male converts were related to prior members of their
churches (computed from surnames within congregations).
Traditionalists considered Finney's practice of having women
and men pray together the most dangerous of the new measures, for it implied new kinds of equality between the sexes.
Indeed some harried husbands recognized the revival as sub-
versive of their authority over their wives. A man calling
himself Anticlericus complained of Finney's visit to his home:

> He *stuffed* my wife with tracts, and alarmed her fears, and
> nothing short of meetings, night and day, could atone for the
> many fold sins my poor, simple spouse had committed, and at
> the same time, she made the miraculous discovery, that she had
> been "unevenly yoked." From this unhappy period, peace,
> quiet, and happiness have fled from my dwelling, never, I fear,
> to return.[29]

The evangelicals assigned crucial religious duties to wives and
mothers. In performing those duties, women rose out of old
subordinate roles and extended their moral authority within
families. Finney's male converts were driven to religion because they had abdicated their roles as eighteenth-century
heads of households. In the course of the revival, their wives
helped to transform them into nineteenth-century husbands.[30]

A SHOPKEEPER'S MILLENNIUM

Charles Finney's revival enlarged every Protestant church, broke down sectarian boundaries, and mobilized a religious community that had at its disposal enormous economic power. Motives which determined the use of that power derived from the revival, and they were frankly millenarian.

As Rochester Protestants looked beyond their community in 1831, they saw something awesome. For news of Finney's revival had helped touch off a wave of religious enthusiasm throughout much of the northern United States. The revival moved west into Ohio and Michigan, east into Utica, Albany, and the market towns of inland New England. Even Philadelphia and New York City felt its power.[31] Vermont's congregational churches grew by 29 percent in 1831. During the same twelve months the churches of Connecticut swelled by over a third.[32] After scanning reports from western New York, the Presbyterian General Assembly announced in wonder that "the work has been so general and thorough, that the whole customs of society have changed."[33] Never before had so many Americans experienced religion in so short a time. Lyman Beecher, who watched the excitement from Boston, declared that the revival of 1831 was the greatest revival of religion that the world had ever seen.[34]

Rochester Protestants saw conversions multiply and heard of powerful revivals throughout Yankee Christendom. They saw divisions among themselves melt away, and they began to sense that the pre-millennial unanimity was at hand—and that they and people like them were bringing it about. They had converted their families and neighbors through prayer. Through ceaseless effort they could use the same power to convert the world. It was Finney himself who told them that "if they were united all over the world the Millennium might be brought about in three months."[35] He did not mean that Christ was coming to Rochester. The immediate and gory millennium predicted in Revelation had no place in evangelical thinking. Utopia would be realized on earth, and it would be made by God with the active and united collaboration of His people. It was not the physical reign of Christ that Finney predicted but the reign of Christianity. The millennium would be accomplished when sober, godly men—men whose every step was guided by a living faith in Jesus—exercised power in this world. Clearly, the revival of 1831 was a turning point in the long struggle to establish that state of affairs. American Protestants knew that, and John Humphrey Noyes later recalled that "in 1831, the whole orthodox church was in a state of ebullition in regard to the Millennium."[36] Rochester evangelicals stood at the center of that excitement.

After 1831 the goal of revivals was the christianization of the world. With that at stake, membership in a Protestant church entailed new kinds of personal commitment. Newcomers to Brick Presbyterian Church in the 1820s had agreed to obey the laws of God and of the church, to treat fellow members as brothers, and "to live as an humble Christian." Each new convert was told that "renouncing all ungodliness and every worldly lust, you give up your all, soul and body, to be the Lord's, promising to walk before him in holiness and love all the days of your life."[37] Not easy requirements, certainly, but in essence personal and passive. With the Finney revival, the ingrown piety of the 1820s turned outward and aggressive. In 1831 Brick Church rewrote its covenant, and every member signed this evangelical manifesto:

We [note that the singular "you" has disappeared] do now, in the presence of the Eternal God, and these witnesses, covenant to be the Lord's. *We promise to renounce all the ways of sin, and to make it the business of our life to do good and promote the declarative glory of our heavenly Father.* We promise steadily and devoutly to attend upon the institutions and ordinances of Christ as administered in this church, and to submit ourselves to its direction and discipline, until our present relation shall be regularly dissolved. We promise to be kind and affectionate to all the members of this church, to be tender of their character, and to endeavor to the utmost of our ability, to promote their growth in grace. *We promise to make it the great business of our life to glorify God and build up the Redeemer's Kingdom in this fallen world*, and constantly to endeavor to present our bodies a living sacrifice, holy and acceptable to Him.[38]

In that final passage, the congregation affirmed that its actions —both individually and in concert—were finally meaningful only in relation to the Coming Kingdom. Everything they did tended either to bring it closer or push it farther away.

Guiding the new activism was a revolution in ideas about human ability. The Reverend William James of Brick Church had insisted in 1828 that most men were innately sinful. Christians could not change them, but only govern their excesses through *"a system of moral regulations, founded upon the natural relations between moral beings, and having for its immediate end the happiness of the community."*[39] We have seen, however, that certain of those "natural relations" were in disarray, and that the businessmen and master workmen who were expected to govern within them were the most active participants in the revival. Evangelical theology absolved them of responsibility by teaching that virtue and order were products not of external authority but of choices made by morally responsible individuals. Nowhere, perhaps, was this put more simply than in the Sunday schools. In the 1820s children had been taught to read and then forced to memorize huge parts of the Bible. (Thirteen-year-old Jane Wilson won a prize in 1823 when she committed a numbing 1,650 verses to memory.)[40] After 1831 Sunday-school scholars stopped memorizing the Bible. The object now was to have them study a few verses a week and to come to an understanding of them, and thus to prepare themselves for conversion and for "an active and useful Christian life."[41] Unregenerate persons were no longer to be disciplined by immutable authority and through fixed social relationships. They were free and redeemable moral agents, accountable for their actions, capable of accepting or rejecting God's promise. It was the duty of Christian gentlemen not to govern them and accept responsibility for their actions but to educate them and change their hearts.

William Wisner, pastor at Brick Church during these years, catalogued developments that were "indispensably necessary to the bringing of millennial glory." First, of course, was more revivals. Second, and tied directly to the first, was the return of God's people to the uncompromising personal standards of the primitive Christians and Protestant martyrs.[42] For the public and private behavior of converts advertised what God had done for them. If a Christian drank or broke the Sabbath or cheated his customers or engaged in frivolous conversation, he weakened not only his own reputation but the awesome cause he represented. While Christian women were admonished to discourage flattery and idle talk and to bring every conversation onto the great subject, troubled businessmen were actually seen returning money to families they had cheated.[43] Isaac Lyon, half-owner of the Rochester Woolen Mills, was seen riding a canal boat on Sunday in the fall of 1833. Immediately he was before the trustees of his church. Lyon was pardoned after writing a confession into the minutes and reading it to the full congregation. He confessed that he had broken the eighth commandment. But more serious, he admitted, was that his sin was witnessed by others who knew his standing in the church and in the community, and for whom the behavior of Isaac Lyon reflected directly on the evangelical cause. He had shamed Christ in public and given His enemies cause to celebrate.[44]

Finney's revival had, however, centered among persons whose honesty and personal morals were beyond question before they converted. Personal piety and circumspect public behavior were at bottom means toward the furtherance of revivals. At the moment of rebirth, the question came to each of them: "Lord, what wilt thou have me do?" The answer was obvious: unite with other Christians and convert the world. The world, however, contained bad habits, people, and institutions that inhibited revivals and whose removal must precede the millennium. Among church members who had lived in Rochester in the late 1820s, the right course of action was clear. With one hand they evangelized among their own unchurched poor. With the other they waged an absolutist and savage war on strong drink.

On New Year's Eve of the revival winter, Finney's co-worker Theodore Weld delivered a four-hour temperance lecture at First Presbyterian Church. Weld began by describing a huge open pit at his right hand, and thousands of the victims of drink at his left. First he isolated the most hopeless—the runaway fathers, paupers, criminals, and maniacs—and marched them into the grave. He moved higher and higher into society, until only a few well-dressed tipplers remained outside the grave. Not even these were spared. While the audience rose to its feet the most temperate drinkers, along with their wives and helpless children, were swallowed up and lost. Weld turned to the crowd and demanded that they not only abstain from drinking and encourage the reform of others but that they unite to stamp it out. They must not drink or sell liquor, rent to a grogshop, sell grain to distillers, or patronize merchants who continued to trade in ardent spirits. They must, in short, utterly disengage from the traffic in liquor and use whatever power they had to make others do the same. A packed house stood silent.[45]

The Reverend Penney rose from his seat beside the Methodist and Baptist preachers and demanded that vendors in the audience stop selling liquor immediately. Eight or ten did so on the spot, and the wholesale grocers retired to hold a meeting of their own. The next day Elijah and Albert Smith, Baptists who owned the largest grocery and provisions warehouse in the city, rolled their stock of whiskey out onto the sidewalk.

While cheering Christians and awestruck sinners looked on, they smashed the barrels and let thousands of gallons of liquid poison run out onto Exchange Street.[46]

Within a week, Everard Peck wrote home that "the principal merchants who have traded largely in ardent spirits are about abandoning this unholy traffic & we almost hope to see this deadly poison expelled from our village."[47] The performance of the Smith brothers was being repeated throughout Rochester. Sometimes wealthy converts walked into groceries, bought up all the liquor, and threw it away. A few grocers with a fine taste for symbolism poured their whiskey into the Canal. Even grocers who stayed outside the churches found that whiskey on their shelves was bad for business. The firm of Rossiter and Knox announced that it was discontinuing the sale of whiskey, but "not thinking it a duty to 'feed the Erie Canal' with their property, offer to sell at cost their whole stock of liquors . . ."[48] Those who resisted were refused advertising space in some newspapers,[49] and in denying the power of a united evangelical community they toyed with economic ruin. S. P. Needham held out for three years, but in 1834 he announced that he planned to liquidate his stock of groceries, provisions, and liquors and leave Rochester. "Church Dominancy," he explained, "has such influence over this community that no honest man can do his own business in his own way . . ."[50]

Almost immediately, Weld's absolutist temperance pledge became a condition of conversion—the most visible symbol of individual rebirth.[51] The teetotal pledge was only the most forceful indication of church members' willingness to use whatever power they had to coerce others into being good, or at least to deny them the means of being bad. While whiskey ran into the gutters, two other symbols of the riotous twenties disappeared. John and Joseph Christopher, both of them new Episcopalians, bought the theater next door to their hotel, closed it, and had it reopened as a livery stable. The Presbyterian Sprague brothers bought the circus building and turned it into a soap factory. Increasingly, the wicked had no place to go.[52]

These were open and forceful attacks on the leisure activities of the new working class, something very much like class violence. But Christians waged war on sin, not workingmen. Alcohol, the circus, the theater, and other workingmen's entertainments were evil because they wasted men's time and clouded their minds and thus blocked the millennium. Evangelicals fought these evils in order to prepare society for new revivals. It was missionary work, little more. And in the winter following Finney's departure, it began to bear fruit.

6
Christian Soldiers

WITH one arm evangelicals attacked the bad habits and tawdry amusements of unregenerate workingmen. With the other they offered redemption. They invited humbler men into their churches. They poured money into poor congregations, financed the establishment of new churches in working-class neighborhoods, and used their wealth and social position to help poor but deserving brethren. By the middle 1830s hundreds of workingmen were in the churches and participating in middle-class crusades.

MISSIONS

While Finney was still in town, rich evangelicals met to organize a church for canal workers, transients, and Rochester's unchurched poor. The committee was headed by Jonothan Child, the most active Episcopal layman in Rochester, and it included rich men from every church. The new congregation was to be a "free" church which abolished pew rents in an attempt to erase class distinctions among the membership. Organized in 1832 as Free Presbyterian Church, this mission was an enormous success. The founding congregation numbered only 45 persons, most of them wealthy members from older Presbyterian churches. At the end of one year, the membership had swelled to 237.[1] Inspired by this success, members of old churches founded Second Baptist and Bethel Presbyterian as free congregations in the mid-1830s. In these churches some of the wealthiest men in Rochester brought their families to worship in fellowship with newly pious day laborers, boatmen, and journeyman craftsmen.[2]

At the same time Finney's converts assisted the older working-class churches in every way they could. First Methodist—made up overwhelmingly of workingmen and their families—was the largest congregation in Rochester by 1834, and much of that growth was made possible by the benevolence of wealthy evangelicals. Twice in the 1830s that unlucky congregation saw its church burn to the ground. After the fire of 1832, the Methodists obtained a loan from the bank at Hartford, recommended and countersigned by rich Presbyterians.[3] When the church caught fire in 1834, Methodists held an open meeting in the courthouse square, attended by ministers and laymen of every denomination. They passed the hat and received enough money to build another new church.[4] The little knot of Freewill Baptists who began meeting at the courthouse in 1836 also enjoyed revival-induced benevolence. While dividing Sundays between his congregation and the inmates of the county jail, the minister remarked, "We are treated with much kindness by all classes, and especially by all evangelical Christians." His remarks took on weight two months later, when a member of Third Presbyterian Church gave him a thousand dollars to build a meetinghouse.[5]

Even the smallest and most despised congregations could look to Finney's converts for help. The African Methodist Church had been built in 1827 with donations from white church members, but in the 1830s that church was financially troubled. The leading trustee and the man most frequently chosen as spokesman for the Rochester black community was Austin Steward, a Main Street grocer. Steward spent his profits on the church and on the unsuccessful Wilberforce Colony in Canada. By the middle 1830s both he and his congregation were bankrupt. But Steward had been in Rochester since 1817, and he had old friends among white evangelicals.

He had also been among the first of the smaller grocers to stop
selling liquor. Wealthy Presbyterians organized and provided
him with interest-free loans, free legal advice, and promises of
exclusive patronage. And when the temperance society organized a huge non-alcoholic Fourth of July picnic in 1837, it was
Austin Steward who received the catering contract. Within a
year, both Steward and the African Methodists were back on
their feet.[6]

Simultaneously, evangelicals established institutions to encourage workingmen to reform themselves and to sustain
those who reformed. In 1831 rich church members founded the Rochester Savings Bank to encourage working-class thrift and personal discipline, and served without pay on its
board of directors.[7] At the same time the congregations at First
Presbyterian, St. Luke's Episcopal, and Free Presbyterian
Churches organized schools to teach reading, writing, and
proper thoughts to poor children, and to keep them away from
"the highways and resorts of dissipation."[8] The parents of
these children had to contend with the wealthy women who
organized the Female Charitable Society, and who went door-
to-door in poor neighborhoods determining which families
needed help and which deserved it. Work was scarce during
the winter months, and unpredictable even during busy times.
With the exceptions of the dreaded almshouse and, of course,
the churches themselves, this society of Christian women was
the only relief organization in Rochester.[9]

Evangelicals encouraged working-class churches and
churchmembers not out of pity or as an attempt to bribe
workingmen but to build up the Kingdom of Christ in Rochester. They were enormously successful. In 1832 trustees at Second Presbyterian invited the evangelist Jedediah Burchard
into their church. Burchard was a crude, half-educated man
and a powerful preacher, and he drew a new kind of audience.[10] Word moved quickly, and the revival spread again to
every church. Baptist, Methodist, Presbyterian, and Episcopal

ministers preached from the same pulpit, and the place of meeting shifted indiscriminately between churches. In the following year and again in 1836, Rochester ministers repeated the performance without outside help. These were powerful revivals. In many congregations—First Methodist, Second Presbyterian, and a growing number of new churches—the revivals of the middle 1830s dwarfed Finney's earlier triumph. "It begins," stated one of Finney's busy converts, "to look like the millennium . . ."[11]

Enthusiasm generated in 1831 was moving into new places. For while businessmen and master craftsmen and their families continued to join churches in the 1830s, they did so in the company of large numbers of wage earners. In 1830–31 journeyman craftsmen had accounted for only 22 percent of male converts—half their proportion of the male work force. Burchard wakened the workingmen, and in subsequent years middle-class missionaries converted hundreds of wage-earning Rochesterians. A full 42 percent of the men who joined churches between 1832 and 1837 were journeyman craftsmen.[12] The workingman's revival was in fact much larger than can be demonstrated systematically, for available evidence seriously underestimates the number of working-class converts. The records of some poor churches—First Methodist and Free Presbyterian in particular—are incomplete. And city directories excluded the most transient and thus generally the youngest and poorest men. These sources identify one in seven journeymen in 1837 as Protestant church members. Were records complete, it is likely that the figure would rise to one in four.[13]

The revivals of 1832–36 were results of middle-class missions, and the churches that benefited from them were without exception middle-class organizations.[14] We are thus left with the question why hundreds of wage earners allied themselves with bourgeois evangelism in the 1830s. Missionaries thought they knew the answer: revivals, they claimed, separated workingmen who were capable of discipline and self-restraint from those who were not.

They were, of course, mistaken. Many wage earners rejected strong drink and riotous amusements as vehemently as they rejected the middle class and its religion. The best bootmakers in Rochester were tramping journeymen from New York City. These independent craftsmen read widely and debated skillfully and defiantly—often on religious subjects— and they avoided excessive drinking and discouraged it in others.[15] Among workingmen who stayed in Rochester, there is ample evidence that individual and group discipline could sustain resistance as well as pious docility. In 1833 journeyman carpenters struck for a ten-hour day, and they protected their strike by telling newcomers to come to them rather than to masters in search of jobs. They met with some success, for at one point all but two contractors agreed to their terms.[16] The carpenters fought the same battle annually until 1836, and there were similar organizations among stonemasons, boat builders, coopers, and calkers.[17] These were orderly, sustained, and well-planned contests with employers, and it is doubtful that they could have been conducted by a working class made up of drunkards and degenerates.

Thus the division between "rough" and "respectable" workingmen did not simply separate those who went to church from those who did not.[18] Of nine leaders of journeymen's societies whose names are known, none belonged to a Protestant church. Indeed many workmen, drawing on traditions of republican skepticism that stretched back to the Revolution, openly opposed the churches. Celebrations of Thomas Paine's birthday were working-class festivals in the middle 1830s, and Rochester was among the few cities outside the old seaports that supported free-thought newspapers. Along with anti-evangelical diatribes and formal disproofs of the existence of God, the free-thought editors printed essays in support of strikes and suggestions that workingmen needed education and self-respect, not middle-class temperance sermons. Paine himself, we may recall, had combined irreligion with calls for education, and with active opposition to violent sports and heavy drinking.[19] There was more than one road to self-improvement in the 1830s.

Why, then, did so many wage earners take the road pointed out by their masters? Some—perhaps most—were already tied to the business community. Many were sons and younger brothers of Finney's middle-class converts, and no doubt many others were trusty employees who followed their masters into church. Still others may have been drawn to evangelists who proclaimed a spiritual rather than a worldly aristocracy among men, and who directed some of their assaults upon the rich and powerful.[20] But with all of this said, the most powerful source of the workingman's revival was the simple, coercive fact that wage earners worked for men who insisted on seeing them in church. In 1836 a free-thought editor announced that clerks were being forced to attend revival meetings. He quoted one of them: "I don't give a d——n. I get five dollars more in a month than before I got religion."[21] We shall see that he was not alone.

REWARDS

"We hope," wrote a Baptist editor in 1834, "the time will come when men will have done employing intemperate mechanics, and when ardent spirits will cease to distract, disturb, and ruin."[22] His hopes were based on the new willingness of Christian employers to demand not only hard work but personal piety of their employees. In the spring of 1831, William Howell completed work on one of the largest and most elegant packet boats ever put on the canal. The job employed thirty boat builders, and Howell announced with satisfaction that it was completed "without the stimulus of ardent spirits or liquid poison."[23] Lewis Selye, a young convert who began manufacturing fire engines in 1833, advertised work for machinists, but noted that "none need apply except those of moral habits and the best of workmen."[24] Applicants at the Rochester Woolen Mills (which hired one of the largest work forces in town) were told that they "must be of moral and temperate habits . . ."[25] The iron founders Thomas Kempshall and John Bush owned another establishment that hired large numbers of men. They commented on their position for a machinist and patternmaker that "a man of steady habits will find it a pleasant situation," and added that "none but temperate men need apply."[26]

In the 1830s Christian employers announced that only sober, God-fearing applicants need knock at their doors. The effect of that attempt to impose religious standards on the labor market can be measured partially and indirectly through analysis of population mobility. For if a workman established a fixed home in Rochester, his rootedness may have meant many things. But first of all it meant that he had found steady work.[27] An analysis of residential stability among churchgoing and non-churchgoing wage earners between 1834 and 1838 suggests strongly that workingmen who did not join churches had trouble finding jobs. Churchgoing clerks were twice as stable as non-churchgoers in the same occupation. Among journeymen and laborers, churchgoers were three-and-one-half times as likely to stay in town as were non-church members. These relationships persist, it should be noted, when they are controlled for age, property holdings, and length of prior residence. Workmen who went to church became settled residents of Rochester *because* they went to church. Their non-churchgoing workmates stayed a few months or years and then moved on to other, perhaps friendlier, towns.[28]

Church membership played an equally powerful role in selecting those wage earners who rose to the ownership of their own stores and workshops.[29] Opportunities for journeymen shrank during these years. In 1827, 16 percent of all men in skilled blue-collar occupations owned workshops. Within the next ten years that figure dropped to 11 percent. Simple arithmetic told journeymen that few of them could hope to become master craftsmen. Yet over half the churchgoing journeymen completed that step. Among their non-churchgoing workmates, the comparable figure was less than one in five—and this among the tiny minority who stayed in Rochester. There was a similar pattern among laborers. By 1837 one man in three possessed little or no skill and depended for his livelihood upon casual, scarce, and low-paying work. For those who wished to move up, the most sensible step was to acquire skills and thus move into better-paying and more secure employment. Two-thirds of the laborers who joined churches made that step between 1827 and 1837. Non-church members in the same occupation moved out of Rochester three times as often, and those who stayed rose at about half the rate attained by church members.

The pattern was identical among clerks. In the 1830s a position as clerk was no longer a stepping-stone to the ownership of a substantial business. More and more had to settle for a small store or for permanent wage-earning status. Few completed the step from clerk to merchant. Most of those who did belonged to Protestant churches. Of the clerks who joined churches during the revivals and who remained in Rochester in 1837, 72 percent became merchants, professionals, or shopkeepers. Most non-churchgoing clerks left Rochester. Of those who stayed, half skidded into blue-collar jobs.

While it varied between occupations, the relation between occupational advancement and membership in a church was strong throughout the wage-earning population. A full 63 percent of churchgoing wage earners who stayed in Rochester between 1827 and 1837 improved their occupational standing. Only 2 percent (one man) declined. Most of the non-church members who worked beside them in 1827 did not stay long enough to have their occupations measured twice. The few who did advanced about half as often as did church members, and they were six times as likely to decline.

The most stable and successful workmen in Rochester were those who went to church. That much can be demonstrated in a systematic way. But the reasons why church members prospered while non-church members moved away or stagnated are not so easily counted. The most obvious explanation is that membership in a church induced habits and attitudes that fit comfortably with a market economy and a disciplined work environment. It is likely that churchgoers were objectively better workers than others, that they worked hard and saved their money, and that they came to the shop sober and on time. No doubt those qualities were crucial to their success. But they were useless until other men decided to reward them. In Rochester no man made his way alone. Whether his career prospered or went sour depended on decisions made by others: decisions to hire him, to promote him, to enter into partnership with him, and to recommend him to neighbors and friends. Social mobility was a social product, and patterns of mobility cannot be explained apart from the means by which individual successes and failures were brought about. Here it will be helpful to trace the entry of individual converts into the business community in the 1830s. We shall find—and it should come as no surprise—that their mobility was directly sponsored by the churchgoing elite.

The carpenter Lauren Parsons took the simplest route. He joined his employer's church in 1831, and went into partnership with him the following year.[30] There were others who did the same. Of the thirty-one wage-earning converts who went into business in the 1830s, sixteen did so in partnership with others. Only four joined with relatives, suggesting that, like Lauren Parsons, they were indeed recruited from outside the old business-owning families.[31] Ten of the sixteen, however, entered business in partnership with other church members—eight of them with members of their own congregations. Here was the most direct kind of sponsorship.

But the career of Lewis Selye suggests that aid to aspiring converts went far beyond formal partnerships. In 1827 Selye was a propertyless journeyman blacksmith. Ten years later he was sole proprietor of a machine shop and fire-engine factory, and one of the richest men in Rochester. An editor described Selye's factory as "a compliment to the ingenuity and enterprise of our townsman . . . who has established this and other branches of business through the force of his own skill and perseverence, unaided by any stock companies or capitalists."[32] True, Selye never formed a partnership. But he had help nonetheless. Decisions that paved the way for Lewis Selye's success were made by the town fathers themselves. He built his first fire engine in 1833 at the request of the village trustees—four months after he joined Brick Presbyterian Church. The same city officials, all of them rich church members, lent their prestigious endorsements to his advertisements.[33]

Despite this assistance, the road was not always smooth for Lewis Selye. In 1837 a sharp decline in orders forced him to close the shop. He sold the business to Martin Briggs, a member of his church and an in-law of the powerful Scrantom family.[34] But the transaction was never put on paper. Lewis Selye appeared as an engine builder in the directory compiled months later, and he continued throughout the 1840s as a successful manufacturer and Whig politician, and as a trustee of Brick Church. It appears that Martin Briggs had not bought him out in 1837. He had bailed him out.

Alvah Strong was another young man who reaped material as well as spiritual rewards from his association with the churches. Strong's father was a doctor and boardinghouse keeper whose clientele consisted first of laborers who dug the canal, then of Rochester workingmen. His brother owned a small candy and fruit store on Exchange Street. The Strongs were not a rich family, but their early and continuous residence in Rochester and their prominence within the Baptist Church (the father was one of the oldest members, the brother was superintendent of the Sunday school) gained them entry into the town's church-bounded community of respectability. Alvah Strong wanted to be a newspaperman. He served an apprenticeship on one Rochester weekly and worked as foreman on another in the 1820s. Then he traveled through the state working as a journeyman. In 1831 Erastus Shepard, a former employer, moved to Rochester and bought the *Anti-Masonic Enquirer*. He offered Alvah Strong a partnership, largely because Strong's "knowledge of the place, and familiarity with the people would strengthen the concern." Strong and Shepard both converted during the Finney revival. Neither had much money, and for the first few years they operated the paper on credit. "Our good name and our industry," Strong explained, "were our capital, so that we commanded credit when it was needed." Most of the money came from wealthy evangelicals who, in 1834, financed the *Enquirer*'s transition into a Whig daily.[35]

Alvah Strong and Lewis Selye earned the friendship of rich evangelicals not only by joining their churches but by living up to Christian standards and enforcing them on others. Selye became a leading layman at Brick Church, and he demanded total abstinence of the men who worked for him. And there were no more consistent temperance editorializers than Alvah Strong and Erastus Shepard. Here, obviously, were men upon whom Christian money was well spent.

There were, of course, converts who began new lives and then slid backward. These found that the churches could dispense punishments as well as rewards. John Denio was a young printer who moved to Rochester in 1833, joined Brick Presbyterian Church, and bought the *Rochester Gem* from his fellow communicant Edwin Scrantom. During the following summer, he was seen in a hotel bar joking and drinking wine with a group of traveling salesmen. When called before the trustees of his church (yes, Lewis Selye was among them), Denio angrily denied that he had done anything wrong. He was excommunicated on the spot. Within a year, the *Gem* had been taken over by Shepard and Strong, and its ruined editor had disappeared from Rochester.[36] Ela Burnap, an old resident of the town, experienced a similar fall from grace. In 1830 he was a master silversmith and the owner of a house on North Fitzhugh, the most uniformly wealthy block in the city. But two years later, another church member saw him drunk. He was suspended from his church. Unlike John Denio, Burnap stayed in Rochester. In 1837 the tax assessor found him working as a watchmaker and living in a rented house on the outskirts of town.[37]

Charles Finney's revival mobilized economic power in Rochester and injected religious motives into its use. The careers of Lewis Selye, Alvah Strong, John Denio, and Ela Burnap reflect that fact. In the 1830s men seeking jobs and credit knocked at the doors of businessmen pushed by their changed souls and by enormous social pressure to prepare Rochester for the millennium. By dispensing and withholding patronage, Christian entrepreneurs regulated the membership of their own class, and to a large extent of the community as a whole. Conversion and abstinence from strong drink became crucial economic credentials. For membership in a church and participation in its crusades put a man into the community in which economic decisions were made, and at a time when religious criteria dominated those choices. By the middle 1830s there were two working classes in Rochester: a churchgoing minority tied closely to the sources of steady work and advancement, and a floating majority that faced insecure employment and stifled opportunities.

In the late 1820s Rochester had divided bitterly along ideological and class lines. Charles Finney's revival melted the first of those divisions, and subsequent enthusiasms transformed the second. Now society split starkly between those who loved Jesus and those who did not. In 1833 a Presbyterian woman walked through a poor neighborhood with her maid, an Irish girl who had quit the Catholic Church and joined with the Presbyterians. Apparently they were insulted in the street. The woman went home and wrote, "The work of the Lord among Christians deepens in some & others grow bolder in opposition. There will soon be two parties . . ."[38]

CHRISTIAN POLITICS

In the spring of 1834, seven men met in the offices of the *Anti-Masonic Enquirer* and formed the Whig Party in Rochester. Representing the Antimasons were Frederick Whittlesey, Timothy Childs, E. Darwin Smith—all of them Episcopalians —and the Presbyterian Harvey Ely. Across the table sat Jesse Hawley and Jonothan Child, both of them Bucktails and Masons, and both of them communicants at St. Luke's Church. These men had fought each other bitterly in the late 1820s, both in village politics and within their troubled congregation. Acting as peacemaker was Alvah Strong, co-owner of the *Enquirer*. The son of a Rochester physician, Strong's experiences with the political troubles of the 1820s had been intimate. He had known William Morgan, for that unfortunate man had been his father's patient and a boarder in his house. Strong's father and brother were Antimasons, and young Alvah had served his apprenticeship under the Antimasonic printer Edwin Scrantom. Then, in 1829, he became foreman on *The Craftsman* and extended his circle of friends to the wealthy Masons whom that paper defended. In 1831 Strong witnessed and participated in Charles Finney's revival. So had the other six men in his office that day. With the meeting finished, the Baptist Alvah Strong and his Presbyterian partner, with money from five Episcopalians and from Harvey Ely of First Presbyterian Church, began printing the *Daily Democrat* as the Whig organ in Rochester.[39]

Over the next few months Whigs and their Democratic opponents built a party system that conformed to social divisions created in the Rochester revival. Whigs filled their organization with wealthy men from every church in town. Fully 63 percent of Whig candidates and campaigners between 1834 and 1837 were merchants, professionals, and master workmen. Among the Democrats, the comparable figure was 46 percent. Thirty-two percent of Whigs and only 19 percent of Democrats ranked in the richest tenth of taxpayers. But Whigs were not simply the party of businessmen. They were the party of Protestant Christians. Sixty-four percent of Whig activists were full church members. (Five years earlier, remember, only one in five Antimasonic and Democratic campaigners was a Protestant communicant.) Only 36 percent of Democrats belonged to Protestant churches, and many of these huddled together at St. Paul's Episcopal, where High Church ritual and the fellowship of other Democrats insulated them from Whig evangelicals.[40]

The meeting in Alvah Strong's office and the party machine that resulted from it embodied a startling reconciliation of differences among the churchgoing elite. That reconciliation stemmed directly from the revival of 1831. Veterans of the old Clintonian and Antimasonic factions, legitimate ancestors of the Whigs, moved almost unanimously into the new party. Temperance men did the same. So did Sabbatarians, whose unpopular stance of 1829 had gained legitimacy within the churches and hence, as we shall see, within the Whig Party. Democrats, of course, remained Democrats. But four in ten anti-Sabbatarians forgot their old worries about religious control and joined with the Whigs. Most striking of all were the new affiliations of Masons and Bucktail Republicans. These men had experienced proscription at first hand, and their old enemies the Antimasons dominated the new coalition. The non-church members among them stayed out of the Whig Party. But of Masons who belonged to Protestant churches, more than half joined with the Whigs. Among churchgoing

Bucktails, the figure was a full three-fourths.[41] There is no more powerful testimony to the social and emotional transformation wrought in Charles Finney's revival.

The first test of the Whig Party came quickly. After years of refusals, the New York legislature incorporated Rochester as a city in 1834. The city charter granted broad powers, including the appointment of a mayor and most other officials, to a common council consisting of an alderman and assistant from each of the five wards. Other than an $8,000 tax limit, there were few brakes on the powers of the council. Aldermen could do what they wanted with the controversial licensing issue. The charter was received in April, and the first city elections were set for June.[42]

It was clear that temperance would be the key issue. In 1832, on the heels of the Finney revival, Antimasonic trustees had raised the price of grocery licenses and for the first time looked into the moral qualifications of applicants. They granted only twenty-eight licenses that year, little more than a quarter of what previous governments had dispensed.[43] That, along with the Antimasons' inability to win a city charter from Democrats in the legislature, led to their defeat in 1833. The incoming Democratic board refused to consider the question of licensing, and grocers all over the city operated without official sanction and without interference.[44] Democrats had begun to present themselves as an anti-temperance, anti-coercion party, and their new permissiveness was met by the most shocking of the drink-related crimes of the 1820s and 1830s. In September a constable entered an unlicensed grocery to stop a fight, and one of the drunken combatants kicked him in the stomach, rupturing his intestines. He died the next day. That night a citizens' meeting appointed a committee of one hundred vigilantes to enforce the dormant licensing law. The committee was made up overwhelmingly of men who would become Whigs.[45]

In the city elections of 1834, the Whigs ran a slate of radical temperance candidates, and their campaign embodied the new social divisions created in the revival. Whig campaigners were rich church members. They could speak with wage earners only on the job and, increasingly, at church. Democrats, on the other hand, drew more than half their activists from among the workingmen themselves, and from the grocers and petty retailers who served working-class neighborhoods. While Whigs preached temperance from a distance, Democrats fought back from within the neighborhoods where most drinking was done. The Democratic campaign was typified by noisy rallies where, according to the Whigs, "whiskey runs like water," and on election morning a crowd of men paraded through town waving bottles and cheering for the Democrats.[46] Few voters in 1834 misunderstood the connection between the classic hands-off liberalism of Jacksonian democracy and the protection of working-class neighborhoods from evangelical meddling. A Whig campaign worker ventured into the Cornhill slum and asked a woman how her husband planned to vote. He got this as a reply: "Why he has always been Jackson, and I don't think he has joined the Cold Water."[47]

The Whigs won by small majorities in every ward, and a worried Democrat announced that "the work of *regeneration* has commenced—a war of extermination against *Barber poles* and *tavern signs.* "[48] Whigs wanted to issue no grocery licenses at all. But their small majorities convinced them to introduce the abolition of public drinking houses by stages. During 1834 they granted only four licenses, at the prohibitive price of forty and fifty dollars each. At least two of these went to large hotels. In working-class neighborhoods, every drinking establishment had either to close its doors or operate outside the law.

Temperance was again the issue in 1835, and this time Whig intransigence produced a Democratic victory. As Democratic aldermen took their seats, they began issuing scores of new licenses. These were sent to the Whig mayor, Jonothan Child

for his signature. Child refused to sign them, and when reminded of his legal obligation to do so, he resigned, explaining,
"I dare not retain the public station which exposes me to this
unhappy dilemma."[49] The council appointed a committee of
three to respond to Child's resignation. On it were Hestor L.
Stevens, Isaac Elwood, and Matthew Brown: two Democrats
and a moderate Whig. Their response remained Democratic
dogma throughout the decade, and it deserves quotation at
length:

> Your committee, claiming to be considered as friends of the
> cause of "temperance," differ, as they believe a majority of this
> board, as well as a large majority of the citizens of this city do,
> from some of the leading measures which have been pursued
> . . . by many of the friends of the "temperance cause . . ." Your
> committee assume that to traffic in ardent spirits is legitimately
> the natural right of every man who sees fit to do so, although
> the expediency of the thing may well be doubted . . .
>
> Anything which savours of restraint in what men deem their
> natural rights is sure to meet with opposition, and men con-
> vinced of error by force will most likely continue all their lives
> unconvinced in their reason. Whatever shall be done to stay the
> tide of intemperance, and roll back its destroying wave, must
> be done by *suasive* appeals to the reason, the interest, or the
> pride of men; but not by force.
>
> Persuasion, gentle as the dews of heaven, must speak of "bur-
> ied hopes and prospects faded," of ruined fortunes, broken
> hearts, and desolated homes. Fashion, too, must be brought in,
> to exercise her all-powerful influence over deluded man, and to
> restrain him from moral pollution and the yawning gulf of
> perdition; but every effort to restrain or reform him by our
> present laws must prove not only ineffectual, but injurious.[50]

Here was the old argument over means. Mayor Child and
his Whig friends wanted to outlaw liquor. Democrats considered drinking a matter of individual choice and Whig methods
a threat to individual liberties. The Jacksonians were not, as
their opponents claimed, a "whiskey party."[51] Many of them

spoke out against intemperance, and they sometimes took the lead in providing alternative amusements.[52] But they drew the line at attempts to influence noncriminal behavior by force. Hestor Stevens, who helped draft the reply to Child, had been elected secretary of the Monroe County Temperance Society in December 1830. His fellow Democrat Addison Gardiner was chosen president of the Young Men's Temperance Society during the same month. But when the societies took their stands for total abstinence and proscription a few weeks later, Stevens and Gardiner disappeared from the rosters.[53]

Ideological differences between Democrats and Whigs were precisely those that had disrupted politics in the late 1820s. But then the argument took place within a hamstrung elite, and within reform groups that stood outside of politics. When the argument did enter elections, advocates of force almost invariably lost. That changed with the revivals. Beginning among the Antimasonic trustees in 1832 and culminating in the Whig temperance campaign of 1834, the argument over means became the dividing line in electoral politics.

Rich church members led the Whig Party and formulated its program. The question remains how this influential but small group won elections. Happily, there is a means of identifying most Whig voters. In March 1834, Whigs circulated a petition denouncing Andrew Jackson's removal of government deposits from the Bank of the United States. It was signed by 722 men who appeared in the Rochester directory published that year: 76 percent of the Whig vote four months later. Analysis of that document makes it clear that Whigs drew their popular support from evangelical businessmen and masters, and from workingmen who had joined churches within the preceding few years.[54]

The Whigs were strong at the top of society and weak at the bottom. Their petitioners ranged from 81 percent of the mill owners to only 10 percent of day laborers. Clearly, the business community included the greatest concentration of Whig voters. That was due, however, to the fact that most rich men went to church. The relationship varied between occupations, but membership in a Protestant church approximately doubled the likelihood that a proprietor would sign the Whig petition. Among wage earners, church members were two-and-a-half to four times as likely to support the Whigs as were their non-churchgoing workmates. The Whig percentage among churchgoing day laborers was identical to that of non-churchgoing physicians, and that relationship held throughout the electorate: workingmen who went to church supported the Whig Party at about the same rate as proprietors who did not. The Whigs were organized and run by wealthy entrepreneurs. But they were not the party of merchants and masters on election day. They were the party of the Rochester revival.

In the 1820s the Rochester elite had divided on the question whether workingmen could or should be reformed by force. In part the argument stemmed from inherited political and religious values, in part from the fact that politicians faced popular majorities opposed to the use of force. Charles Finney's revival united wealthy men under the banner of proscription. The ensuing workingman's revival provided them with a constituency large enough to enter and win elections. While revival-wrought changes in the job market prevented non-churchgoing workers from meeting residence requirements, stable churchgoers voted for the forcible regulation of their neighbors. Thus the program, the leadership, and the constituency of the Whig Party in Rochester were created in the religious transformation that began in 1830. Passing through in the summer of 1831, the New York City Democrat James Gordon Bennett declared that "there is a union between religion and politics in all this region of the country." Bennett noted the exclusivity of the dominant evangelical sector of the economy and blamed it for what he recognized as an ominous political situation. "This is a religion," he fumed, "like the Jesuits."[55]

From the middle 1830s onward, evangelical Protestantism dominated social and political argument in the northern United States. In everything from raising babies to electing Presidents, church members muted other loyalties and acted as Christians, and non-church members opposed them at every step. Students of voting behavior in particular have noted that development, and the statement that political—and by inference social—divisions after 1830 are explicable in terms of religion and not of social class has become an academic chant.

These studies describe a relationship between religion and political behavior. The preceding pages have sought its origins in the social history of one small city. Students of Protestantism have always noted its peculiar sensitivity to social change. In the absence of a church hierarchy, an authoritative clergy, or an official relationship with the state, the carriers of Protestantism have been laymen, and religious change has reflected social experience. More precisely, it has mirrored the religious needs of dominant groups within congregations.[56] In Rochester those dominant men were entrepreneurs faced with profound disorders in the social relations surrounding work. Charles Finney's revival provided a solution to the social disorder and moral confusion that attended the creation of a free-labor economy. The Whig Party carried that solution into politics.

The Rochester revival was generated in the problem of social class. Given that, it seems unwise to treat religion and class as separate and competing categories of explanation. The problem is not to discover which exerted greater independent influence over behavior, but to define how they made each other in history.

Afterword:
On Cities, Revivals, and Social Control

ALEXIS DE TOCQUEVILLE came to the United States in the spring of 1831. He noted the first day that Americans were a profoundly religious people, and during his travels he asked scores of ministers and laymen why that was so. He always received the same reply: religion was strong in America because it was necessary, and it was necessary because Americans were free. A society with fixed ranks and privileges controls its members and has no need for religion. But a free society must teach men to govern themselves, and there is no greater inducement to self-restraint than belief in God. "Despotism," Tocqueville concluded, "may govern without faith, but liberty cannot."[1]

1

Tocqueville was among the first to link revival religion with the concept of social control. Many have followed, and most of these share his central insight and repeat his central mistakes. The insight is enduring and valuable: in a society that lacked external controls, revivals created order through individual self-restraint. But Tocqueville refused to ground either religion or the social discipline that derived from it in specific social processes and was content to say that religion helps "society" to control its members. With that, he severed the analysis of social control from the question of who controls whom. True, religion can make men perceive society as something more than the social relations and patterns of action that make it up, and thus it can act as a powerful legitimizing force. But too many studies of revivals perform the same function. Analyses of revivals and social control must not simply repeat that "religion" holds "society" together. They must define the ways in which particular religious beliefs reinforce the dominance of particular ruling groups.

The Rochester revival served the needs not of "society" but of entrepreneurs who employed wage labor. And while there are few systematic studies of revivals in other cities, there is reason to believe that the Rochester case was not unique. In towns and cities all over the northern United States, revivals after 1825 were tied closely to the growth of a manufacturing economy. Whitney Cross, in his pathbreaking study *The Burned-Over District*, found that revivals were strong in such manufacturing centers as Rochester, Lockport, and Utica, while the commercial centers of Buffalo and Albany remained quiet.[2] Subsequent studies have reinforced his observation. Canal towns that were devoted to commerce were relatively immune to revivals. So were the old seaport cities. But in mill villages and manufacturing cities, evangelicalism struck as hard as it had at Rochester. The relation between revivals and manufactures gains strength when we turn from cities to individuals, for in urban places of all types, revivals and their related social movements were disproportionately strong among master workmen, manufacturers, and journeyman craftsmen. There were relatively few merchants and clerks among the converts, and even fewer day laborers and transport workers.[3] Clearly, urban revivals in the 1820s and 1830s had something to do with the growth of manufactures.

In the few towns that have been studied over time, revivals followed the same chronology and served the same functions as they had at Rochester. Everywhere, enthusiasm struck first among masters and manufacturers, then spread through them into the ranks of labor. The workingman's revival of the 1830s was effected through missionary churches, temperance and moral reform societies, and Sunday schools that were dominated by rich evangelicals. The religion that it preached was order-inducing, repressive, and quintessentially bourgeois. In no city is there evidence of independent working-class revivals before the economic collapse of 1837.[4] We must conclude that many workmen (the number varied enormously from town to town) were adopting the religion of the middle class, thus internalizing beliefs and modes of comportment that suited the needs of their employers.

The analysis of Rochester, along with evidence from other cities, allows us to hypothesize the social functions of urban revivals with some precision. Evangelicalism was a middle-class solution to problems of class, legitimacy, and order generated in the early stages of manufacturing. Revivals provided entrepreneurs with a means of imposing new standards of work discipline and personal comportment upon themselves and the men who worked for them, and thus they functioned as powerful social controls. But there was more to it than that. For the belief that every man was spiritually free and self-governing enabled masters to present a relationship that denied human interdependence as the realization of Christian ideals. Here we arrive at the means by which revivals served the needs of "society." For we have begun to define the role of religious sanctions in the process whereby a particular historical form of domination could assume legitimacy, and thus could indeed come to be perceived as "society." A significant minority of workingmen participated willingly in that process. And that, of course, is the most total and effective social control of all.

2

This solves the first problem raised by Tocqueville's analysis, but it confronts us with a second: the tendency to deduce the origins of religion from its social functions. Tocqueville stated that religion was strong in America because it created order among free individuals. We have seen that revivals did indeed create order, but only along lines prescribed by an emerging industrial bourgeoisie. Here we enter dangerous territory. For if we infer the causes of revivals from their results, we must conclude that entrepreneurs consciously fabricated a religion that suited their economic and social needs.[5] That would demonstrate little more than our own incapacity to take religion seriously. True, Charles Finney's revival at Rochester helped to solve the problems of labor discipline and social control in a new manufacturing city. But it was a religious solution, addressed to religious problems. The revival will remain unexplained until we know how social problems became translated into specifically religious unrest.

The businessmen and masters in Charles Finney's audience had been born into New England villages in which the roles of husband, father, and employer were intertwined, and they had reconstructed that village order on the banks of the Genesee. In the early years, disorder and insubordination were held in check, for master and wage earner worked together and slept under the same roof. Fights between workmen were rare, and when they occurred masters witnessed the intelligible and personal stream of events that led up to them. Wage earners loafed or drank or broke the Sabbath only with the master's knowledge and tacit consent. When workers lived with proprietors or within sight of them, serious breaches of the peace or of accepted standards of labor discipline were uncommon. At the very least, workingmen were constrained to act like guests, and masters enforced order easily, in the course of ordinary social and economic transactions.

In the few years preceding the revival of 1831, Charles Finney's converts dissolved those arrangements. And as many recent studies have pointed out, that dissolution posed immense problems of work discipline and social order. In the experience of the master, however, it was worse than that. For when a master broke with home-centered relations of production he abdicated his authority as head of a household and as moral governor of society, and thus lost contact with a crucial part of his own identity. Given the money he made and the trouble he caused others, we need not sympathize too much. But if we are to render his turn to religion intelligible, we must understand that he experienced disobedience and disorder as religious problems—problems that had to do not only with safe streets and the efficient production of flour and shoes but with the "rightness" of new relations of production.

It was a dilemma that had no earthly solution. Rochester masters assumed the responsibility to govern wage earners. But at the same time they severed the relationships through which they had always dominated those men. Resistance in the workshops, the failure of the temperance crusade, and the results of elections in the 1820s dramatized what had become an everyday fact of life: workmen no longer listened when proprietors spoke. The authority of Rochester's ruling groups fell away, leaving them with new economic imperatives, old moral responsibilities, and no familiar and legitimate means of carrying them out. Attempts by a minority to reassert control through coercive means failed and, in the course of failing, split the elite and rendered concerted action impossible. It was the moral dilemma of free labor and the political impasse that it created that prepared the ground for Charles Finney.[6]

The revival of 1831 healed divisions within the middle class and turned businessmen and masters into an active and united missionary army. Governing their actions in the 1830s was the new and reassuring knowledge that authoritarian controls were not necessary. For Finney had told them that man is not innately corrupt but only corruptible. There was no need to hold employees or anyone else in relations of direct dependence. Such relations, in fact, prevented underlings from discovering the infinite potential for good that was in each of them. Thus they inhibited individual conversion and blocked the millennium. From 1831 onward, middle-class religion in Rochester aimed not at the government of a sinful mankind but at the conversion of sinners and the perfection of the world.

The missions were a grand success: hundreds of wage earners joined middle-class churches in the 1830s. This pious enclave within the working class provided masters with more than willing workers and votes for Whig repression. Sober, hardworking, and obedient, they won the friendship and patronage of the middle class, and a startling number of them seized opportunities to become masters themselves. These men demonstrated that paternalistic controls could indeed be replaced by piety and voluntary self-restraint: free labor could generate a well-regulated, orderly, just, and happy society. The only thing needed was more revivals of religion. Workmen who continued to drink and carouse and stay away from church were no longer considered errant children; they were free moral agents who had chosen to oppose the Coming Kingdom. They could be hired when they were needed, fired without a qualm when they were not.

Thus a nascent industrial capitalism became attached to visions of a perfect moral order based on individual freedom and self-government, and old relations of dependence, servility, and mutuality were defined as sinful and left behind. The revival was not a capitalist plot. But it certainly was a crucial step in the legitimation of free labor.

Occupational Groups

THIS study looks closely into the experiences and inter-relations of economic groups in Rochester during the "pre-industrial revolution" of the 1820s and 1830s. The questions it addresses and the kinds of research that seemed most likely to produce answers demanded the collapsing of hundreds of occupations and levels of wealth into a few fairly inclusive categories. That was no simple task. Prestige rankings by occupation were useless, for the economy changed much faster than the language. Men who owned furniture factories and shoe shops called both themselves and their employees chairmakers and shoemakers. For this reason a second alternative—the ranking of occupations by mean wealth—was equally inadequate. In 1827 there were shoemakers and carpenters in every assessment decile, merchants in each of the first eight, and men in every occupation with no property at all. The problem called for the building of categories that combined the occupations and wealth of individuals, categories that both facilitated research and corresponded to real divisions in the Rochester work force. In particular, I had to find some means of separating proprietors from men who worked for wages. The following pages describe ways in which that was done.

WHITE-COLLAR OCCUPATIONS

Economic data on individuals came from two sources: tax lists and city directories. Directories list the occupations of adult men. Tax lists provide a means of ranking their property holdings in relation to each other.[1] Among white-collar men, proprietors and wage earners are obvious in most cases: merchants, grocers, and lawyers are proprietors; clerks are employees. But among the proprietors there are great differences in degree. Establishments owned by grocers, for example, range from wholesale provisions warehouses to neighborhood bars. It seems appropriate to establish a line separating wealthy businessmen and professionals from humbler boardinghouse operators and shopkeepers. Table 7 provides the first indication of where that line belongs. Among the top 30 percent of taxpayers, white-collar men account for at least half the total, while below that line their numbers drop sharply. The third-decile line separates most of the men listed as merchants, lawyers, mill owners, druggists, and jewelers from those listed as grocers, boardinghouse operators, and the like.

TABLE 7. DISTRIBUTION OF OCCUPATIONS WITHIN ASSESSMENT DECILES, 1827 (IN PERCENT)

	1	2	3	4	5	6	7	8	9	10
commercial	57	33	43	19	20	19	8	9	3	–
professional	9	17	7	7	5	2	3	12	–	–
clerical	3	5	1	11	5	8	7	5	2	–
skilled manual	31	44	49	58	54	56	56	43	73	43
unskilled manual	–	–	–	4	18	16	25	29	22	56
N*	93	81	72	73	63	63	59	42	41	23

*The number of cases in each decile was derived in the following manner. Property holders were divided into tenths, which initially included 103 men each. They were then traced in the directory compiled eight months earlier. Those who did not appear there were eliminated, while the original deciles were left intact. Among the by-products is an estimate of the relative stability of men possessing varying levels of wealth.

The property holdings of men listed with no occupation tend to verify that line. Most of these were poor and unemployed. Others were young men who had not yet gone to work, or old men who were retired. But some were wide-ranging entrepreneurs. Jonothan Child, for instance, was

listed without an occupation. Yet he owned the largest forwarding company on the Erie Canal, speculated in a wide
variety of commercial ventures with his brothers-in-law,
maintained a thriving legal practice, operated as agent for a
number of New York City insurance companies, and managed
the landholdings of his aging father-in-law, Nathaniel Rochester. Child, of course, appeared among the richest 10 percent of
taxpayers. Another twenty-two men, most of them readily
identifiable as successful businessmen, appeared in the first
three deciles. In the fourth decile, men listed with no occupation disappear from the tax list, and with the exception of one
man, they do not reappear until the eighth. Most were propertyless. It seems clear that the top three deciles separate promoters from men listed with no occupation because they
really had none. Thus throughout this study I used the line
between the third and fourth assessment deciles to draw the
(admittedly imperfect) line between businessmen and petty
proprietors.

The same line helps solve a small problem created by impre-
cise occupational listings. The top three deciles include a few
clerks, teachers, and accountants. Evidently some clerks were
partners in the stores in which they worked, or became so in
the eight months that intervened between the compilations of
the directory and the tax list. Some teachers owned schools,
and a few bookkeepers were independent semiprofessionals. It
seems proper to include those in the top 30 percent of taxpayers with the merchants and lawyers, and to relegate those who
owned less property or no property to the group of clerical
employees.

BLUE-COLLAR OCCUPATIONS

Blue-collar occupations are more troublesome. Here we are
concerned not with differences of degree but with different
kinds of work: we must separate master craftsmen and manufacturers from the men who worked for them. Most men in

every trade were propertyless and are assumed to have been journeymen. The problem is to determine the line separating masters from home-owning journeymen. The first three assessment deciles, we have seen, are composed almost exclusively of proprietors. We may safely assume that craftsmen who owned as much as most merchants and lawyers were shopowners. In the fourth decile, the number of white-collar men drops sharply, while laborers make their first appearance. Clearly, there are wage earners present from the fourth decile down, and any line drawn below that point will include some home-owning workmen among the masters. But the relatively small number of blue-collar men in the first three deciles, as well as the presence of white-collar proprietors in the lower deciles, suggests that many master workmen fell below the top 30 percent. I had to find a line to separate *most* masters from *most* journeymen.

TABLE 8. PERCENT OF HOUSEHOLDS HEADED BY SKILLED WORKMEN WHICH INCLUDED POSSIBLE EMPLOYEES IN 1827

tax decile	building tradesmen	indoor tradesmen
1	67	81
2	50	69
3	33	45
4	40	46
5	26	50
6	21	15
7	32	20
8	36	20
9	21	25
10	—	25

NOTE: "Possible employees" were day laborers and workmen in related trades, i.e., a gunsmith or blacksmith who lived with a gunsmith was a possible employee, a shoemaker or carpenter was not.

Table 8 takes a step in that direction. Although the integration of economic and domestic life was breaking down in 1827, large numbers of workmen continued to live with their em-

ployers. The table lists the percentage of households headed
by craftsmen in each decile that included either laborers or
workmen in trades either related or identical to that of the
householder. A danger here is the confusion of masters with
journeymen who headed their own households and took in
boarders. That problem is heightened considerably by building tradesmen. The directory describes households in December. But the building season ended in late October. (Few men
tried to work outdoors during the Rochester winter.) Thus
few master builders in the table shared their homes with laborers or construction tradesmen in December, while significant
numbers of journeymen rented lodgings to their workmates.
The composition of households offers little help in separating
masters and journeymen in the building trades.

If we limit consideration to indoor craftsmen whose employment was less subject to seasonal fluctuations, Table 8
presents a clear pattern. There is a dramatic and permanent
break between the fifth and sixth deciles: half the men in the
first five deciles shared their homes with wage earners, while
below that line the proportion drops to one in five. That is the
point at which I draw the line between probable masters and
probable journeymen.

It must be stated immediately that some journeymen have
thus become spurious masters, while many smaller master
craftsmen are included among the journeymen. I have inten-
tionally drawn the line a little high, separating the more substantial shopowners from home-owning wage earners and the
smallest proprietors. Table 9 suggests the amount and kinds of
distortion that have resulted. The 1827 directory lists the number of shops in a wide variety of trades. Once partners have
been combined, the first five deciles include either an identical
or a smaller number of owners than there were shops. In all,
the top half of the town's property holders accounts for the
ownership of 73 percent of its indoor workshops, while there
is (in these trades) no overlap in the other direction. The

TABLE 9. PROPORTIONS OF OWNERS OF MANUFACTURING
ESTABLISHMENTS WHO APPEAR IN ASSESSMENT DECILES
1 THROUGH 5 IN 1827

type of establishment	number of shops	number in deciles 1–5*
blacksmith shop	17	11
cooperage	14	10
shoe shop	14	11
printer's shop	6	4
tin and sheet-iron factory	5	2
saddlery	4	4
hat factory	4	3
furniture factory	4	3
soap and candle factory	3	2
clothier's shop	4	4
distillery	2	1
morocco dresser	2	1
paper mill	1	1
mirror maker	1	1
sashmaker	1	1
lastmaker	1	1
pail and tub factory	1	1
nail factory	1	1

*Partnerships (which are specified in the assessment rolls) have been com-
bined. Thus, these figures refer not to the number of proprietors but to the
number of shops whose owners appear in the first five deciles.

number of wage earners in the first five deciles is negligible,
while the poorest fourth of shopowners is buried somewhere
in the lower deciles.

Newspaper advertisements confirm that estimate. I compiled a list of forty-four men who advertised manufacturing
establishments in or before 1827 and who appeared in the
directory published that year. Of these, 82 percent appeared
in the first five tax deciles. Only 5 percent (two men: the
ropemakers John and James Church) appeared in the sixth.
The others either rented workshops for which they were not
taxed or closed their shops and left Rochester between Decem-

ber 1826 and August 1827. Persistence rates suggest that most fall into the latter category. Thus, estimates derived from the number of shops per trade and from the identification of a significant number of master craftsmen lead to very similar conclusions: the first five deciles include the owners of from three-fourths to four-fifths of indoor workshops, while at the same time they include very few wage earners.[2]

Available evidence dictated that the master and journeyman categories be tailored to the indoor trades. But fully 38 percent of the skilled blue-collar work force were building tradesmen, and evidence and means of testing conclusions about them are shadowy at best. Only forty-eight builders appear in the first five deciles, suggesting a ratio of nine skilled workers (and an indeterminate number of laborers) per master builder. That is a large figure, produced in part by deficiencies in the evidence. Shoemakers, tailors, and gunsmiths worked in the same place every day, a place which the master owned and for which he paid taxes. But carpenters, masons, and house painters worked on land and in buildings they did not own, and real-estate holdings are no reliable indicator of their occupational status. No doubt some master builders either rented houses or boarded in hotels, and owned no more than their skills, their business contacts, and their ability to organize and supervise other men. Thus while tax rolls produce reliable lists of master shoemakers and master blacksmiths, their usefulness in creating lists of master builders is decidedly limited. The fifth-decile line results in a very high ratio of journeymen to masters in the building trades. That ratio is open to serious misgivings and cannot be tested in a systematic way.

Still, there is sound reason to believe that these proportions are not wildly inaccurate. Master builders who appear in the first five deciles include large numbers of men known to have been custom contractors. But it was the construction of houses in groups that provided employment for most journeymen, and as often as not that operation was organized and directed by promoters who appear in directories as merchants, millers, lawyers, and so on. The master builders who are buried among the journeymen were probably not masters in the old sense but subcontractors who hired themselves out and who could more accurately be termed foremen.[3] The journeyman and master categories were fitted to the inmates of indoor workshops. But they have produced lists of master builders that, given the organization of their trade in Rochester, are not far from accurate.

CONCLUSION

These combinations of an individual's occupation and wealth divide the adult male work force into six groups:

1. *Businessman-professional.* This group includes all men in white-collar occupations (including mill owners, government officials, clerks, and those listed with no occupation) who rank in the top 30 percent of taxpayers.

2. *Master craftsman-manufacturer.* These include all men listed with skilled manual occupations (including such titles as merchant tailor and shoe dealer, which become more common in the 1834 and 1838 directories) who appear in the top 50 percent of taxpayers.

3. *Shopkeeper-petty proprietor.* This group is composed of all men listed with nonclerical white-collar occupations (including professionals) who were propertyless or who ranked in the bottom 70 percent of taxpayers.

4. *Clerical employee.* This category includes all nonmanual wage earners (clerks, teachers, government officials, bank tellers, accountants) who were propertyless or who ranked in the bottom 70 percent of taxpayers.

5. *Journeyman craftsman.* These include all men in skilled manual occupations who were propertyless or who ranked in
   the bottom 50 percent of taxpayers. We have seen that this
   group includes some foremen and small shopowners.

6. *Laborer-semiskilled.* These are day laborers, teamsters, boatmen, barbers, waiters, and so on, regardless of assessment
   ranking. All were either propertyless or in the bottom 70
   percent of taxpayers. Added to these are men listed with no
   occupation who ranked below the third assessment decile.

It should be clear by now that I do not claim absolute
accuracy for these categories. Throughout the book conclusions derived from them have been tested and amplified
through consideration of individual occupations, individual workshops, and individual men.

Misgivings aside, I believe that these catgories are more
suitable to the study of an expanding preindustrial city
than others that have been tried. In particular, this scale
comes closer to distinguishing proprietors from wage earners. Thus these categories permit analysis of the experiences and interrelations of real economic groups, and not
of abstractions created by and for modern researchers. For
large calculations, these groups can be collapsed to form
more inclusive categories that still make sense: proprietor
and wage earner, for instance, or white collar and blue
collar. Most important for the problems of this study, these
categories permit the comparison of church members and
non-church members (in groups both large enough and
specific enough to yield meaningful results), while holding
combined occupation and property holdings constant. This
scale recreates actual occupations as closely as can be done
with available evidence, and it is adequate to the discovery
of mathematical rates of occupational mobility and movement across space which have become the common fare of

quantitative studies in social history. But that is not their major purpose. They are meant to form the skeleton of a historical account of relations between economic groups in one rapidly expanding preindustrial city.

Rochester Church Records

T HESE pages describe the membership records of Presbyterian, Episcopal, Methodist, and Baptist churches in Rochester and assess effects of gaps in the records and of population mobility upon what is said in the text. In particular, I wish to spell out the effects of transiency and missing records upon the sequence of rich man's to poor man's revivalism described in Chapter VI.

THE RECORDS OF ROCHESTER CHURCHES

First Presbyterian. There are complete session minutes from the founding in 1815 to the present. These provide the name of each incoming member, the date of his or her admission, and whether he or she entered by letter of transfer or by profession of faith. The records are in typescript, and are stored in the office safe at First Presbyterian Church.

Second (Brick) Presbyterian. There are complete session minutes from the founding in December 1825. These provide information identical to that of First Church. The records are in manuscript and are stored in the basement records vault at Brick Presbyterian Church.

Third Presbyterian. The original session minutes have been lost, but a catalogue published in 1832 lists every person admitted to the church from the founding in 1827 to the end of 1831,

noting whether he entered by letter or by profession.[1] Thus
the records are complete through the Finney revival and unavailable after that. They present another problem in that admissions are undated, and they span both the pre-revival and
the Finney years. Nearly all the early members transferred in
from First and Second Churches, and there were few conversions in 1828 and 1829. Thus when members of Third Church
are placed into one of the three time slots, they are placed with
the Finney revival. This was, in fact, the church that invited
Finney to Rochester. The effects of missing records in the
1830s are not serious, for Third Church went into decline soon
after Finney left town, having to sell its building in 1834. The
church had over 500 members in 1831, 402 in 1832, and 247 in
1834.[2] Much of the membership and most of the energy of this
church transferred into Free Presbyterian.

Free Presbyterian. Founded by an interdenominational committee, but staffed at the beginning by former members of
Third Presbyterian, this congregation was a mission to
Rochester's unchurched poor. It disbanded in 1838, and the
session minutes were lost. The only membership record of this
church is a list of the forty-five founders. Within two years the
church grew to almost four hundred members.[3] The lack of
records for this church has without doubt contributed to a
serious underestimate of the number of wage earners who
joined churches in the 1830s.

Reformed Presbyterian. This church was founded immediately after the Finney revival. Sometimes called the Scots
Church or the Covenanters, it was a small congregation made
up of Scots and Irish Presbyterians. The church included
twenty-seven members at its founding and ninety in 1837.
Elders and trustees in that year included four men who
appear in city directories: two day laborers, a cooper, and a
distiller. The last occupation, along with the fact that this

church refused to maintain a Sunday school, suggests that the Covenanters represented immigrant revulsion at some of the excesses of Yankee evangelicals.[4] Records of the church are lost, contributing again to the underestimate of the number of workingmen who belonged to churches in the 1830s.

Bethel Presbyterian. This church was founded in 1836 by former First Church members, most of them wealthy Finney converts. It was a free church, founded from motives similar to those at Free Presbyterian. The congregation remained small throughout the period of this study, reaching fifty in 1837.[5] There are complete session minutes, identical to those at First and Second Presbyterian, in the offices of Central Presbyterian Church.

St. Luke's Episcopal. This church was organized in 1818 by Nathaniel Rochester, his family and friends. The first minister was one of his in-laws; the second was recruited personally by Rochester and his sons. At every point in time, this was the wealthiest church in Rochester. St. Luke's adopted Low Church ritual and participated fully in the revivals of 1827–37.[6] The records are as nearly complete as Episcopal records can be. The first volume of the Parish Register includes dated admissions to communion from 1820 through 1831. Then there is a gap, with a full list of communicants as of the accession of a new minister in 1833. This is followed by dated admissions for the years 1834–38. The Register is in manuscript, and is stored in the basement closet at St. Luke's Church.

St. Paul's Episcopal. The founding of this church and its political leanings are discussed in the text.[7] The records are similar to those at St. Luke's. The Parish Register begins with a list of the founding congregation, then a gap, then dated admissions to communion in 1831–32. This is followed by a full list of communicants as of Christmas 1832, permitting the identification of those who joined between 1827 and 1829. There is another list of communicants in late 1833, dated admissions in the middle 1830s, and one more full list as of March 1839. The register is stored in the offices of St. Paul's Church.

Asbury-First Methodist. The lack of full Methodist records is the most serious gap in the membership data. This was the largest church in Rochester in the 1830s, and its membership was made up of workingmen and their families. Significant records, however, have survived. The Trustees' Book, the Conference Register, and the Stewards' Book name scores of church officers, lay preachers, exhorters, class leaders, and members of church committees throughout the 1820s and 1830s. There was a lot of lay participation in Methodist affairs (a class leader for every twelve members, for instance), and these records include a sizable minority of Rochester Methodists. The records are stored in the kitchen closet at Asbury-First United Methodist Church. Here is an estimate of the proportion of adult male Methodists who appear in these records:

1. In 1834 there were 912 Methodists in Rochester.[8] In other blue-collar churches, about 60 percent of the full members were women, yielding an estimated 365 Methodist men in that year.

2. Many of these did not appear in the 1834 directory because they moved in or out of town before or after that document was compiled, and because coverage in directories was prejudiced in favor of the more stable and thus generally the more well-to-do members of the community. First Baptist, another blue-collar church, published a catalogue of its members in 1838. Only 55 percent of the Baptists listed there appear in the directory published the same year. This leads to an estimated 193 Methodist men hidden somewhere in the 1834 directory.

3. In fact, seventy-two male Methodists appear in that document. This yields an estimated 37 percent as the proportion of male Methodists who appear in both church records and city directories and thus are included in this study. It must be stressed, however, that these men were lay leaders and were no doubt wealthier and more stable than the Methodist rank and file. Complete records of this church would add significantly to the workingman's revival of the 1830s, as the only Methodist revival on record came in 1836.[9]

First Baptist. Baptists began meeting and operating a Sunday school as early as 1818, but they did not build a church until 1823. At that time there were 23 members. At the end of 1826, the figure stood at 85. The church experienced a revival in 1827, and by the end of 1828 the membership had risen to 158. The congregation doubled while Finney was in town, then went into decline as much of the energy generated in the revival went into Second Baptist.[10] The original session minutes have been lost. The Sabbath school records and the annual *Minutes* of the Monroe Baptist Association provide the names of lay leaders in the 1820s and early 1830s. Only thirteen of these appear in the directory compiled in December 1826, but these constituted a surprisingly large part of the male membership at that time. Using the series of calculations developed for Methodist records, at least 60 percent seems a good estimate of the proportion of Baptist men who appear in both church records and directories in the 1820s. The worst gap in Baptist records occurs with the Finney revival; no new members appear in the records, but we know that the church doubled in size. The same skimpy records must suffice until 1838, when the church published a catalogue listing the name and address of every member as of that date.[11] Thus the records at First Baptist are good for the 1820s, nonexistent for the Finney revival, and fair to good for the 1830s.

Second Baptist. This church was organized by seceders from First Baptist in 1834, and was an evangelical, temperance, and antislavery congregation.[12] Records have been lost. There is a list of the founding congregation, and dated admissions of persons who joined in the 1830s and who remained members in 1849 (from the second volume of session minutes). Both of these favor the more stable and well-to-do members of the congregation.

TABLE 10. THE EVANGELICAL CHURCHES OF ROCHESTER, 1815–38[*]

	founding date	members[†] in 1834	status of records
First Presbyterian	1815	450	complete
St. Luke's Episcopal	1818	320	complete
First Methodist	1818	912	partial
First Baptist	1823	300	partial
Second Presbyterian	1825	504	complete
Third Presbyterian	1827	247	partial
St. Paul's Episcopal	1827	105	complete
African Methodist	1827	defunct	none
Reformed Presbyterian	1831	50	none
Free Presbyterian	1832	370	partial
Second Baptist	1834	100	partial
Abyssinian Baptist	1834	unknown	none
Bethel Presbyterian	1836	—	complete
Free Congregational	1836	—	none
Freewill Baptist	1836	—	none
Asbury Methodist	1836	—	partial
African Methodist (restored)	1837	—	none

[*]The table includes only churches affiliated with the four major evangelical denominations. This excludes two Roman Catholic churches and small congregations of German Lutherans and native Quakers.
[†]*Charter and Directory of the City of Rochester* (Rochester, 1834), 17.

There are complete, dated records of admission for only a few congregations (Table 10). For some, there are no records at all. Most missing evidence is from blue-collar churches, producing serious underestimates of the number of working-

men who joined churches during these years. The records
become sparser with the passage of time. They are nonexistent
only for churches founded by or for workingmen after 1832.
Thus figures presented in the text are minimum estimates of
the proportion of church members who worked for wages,
particularly in the 1830s. Without question, complete records
would increase the magnitude of the workingman's revival of
the middle 1830s.

CHURCH RECORDS AND TRANSIENCY

A second problem derives from the instability of Rochester's population. Figures presented in the text demonstrate
that churchgoing workingmen were much more settled than
their non-churchgoing workmates. But even they were a volatile group of men. Figures on the annual turnover of membership can be constructed for three congregations: First and
Second Baptist, and St. Luke's Episcopal (Table 11). In the
1830s about one in four church members at the end of each
year had joined within the preceding twelve months. (The
higher figure at Second Baptist was created by transfers from
First Baptist.) These figures, limited to the revival years, are
not particularly startling. More remarkable are the rates of
outmigration. St. Luke's drew its membership from the wealthiest and most stable elements of the population. Yet more than
one in ten moved out every year. Among the poorer Baptists,
annual outmigration rose to 15 percent. (Again, the higher
figure for First Baptist was created by transfers into Second
Baptist.)

The fluidity of the churchgoing population has distorted
evidence presented in the text, for in most calculations coverage is limited to men who stayed in town long enough to
appear in a city directory. Table 12 suggests the dimensions of
that distortion. In the 1820s, and on into the Finney revival,
church records include large numbers of men who never ap-

TABLE II. ANNUAL TURNOVER IN THREE CONGREGATIONS

	percent added	percent dropped
St. Luke's Episcopal, 1830–36	23.6	11.2
First Baptist, 1828–38	25.2	18.3
Second Baptist, 1834–38	37.1	15.1

SOURCES: St. Luke's Parish Register and *Minutes of the Annual Meeting of the Monroe Baptist Association* (Rochester, annually after 1828).

pear in city directories—numbers that range from one in five to almost half. In every congregation, the number of phantom church members rose after 1832. Those figures lead to the conclusion that over half the men admitted to Rochester churches in the 1830s moved into Rochester, joined a church, and left town within a maximum of four years. Data presented in the text suggest that these included proportionally more workingmen than proprietors. With the number of unknowns increasing after Finney left town, it seems safe to infer that full information would increase the size of the workingman's revival of the 1830s.

Population mobility has had another troublesome effect upon evidence presented in the text. While many church members moved out of Rochester in these years, many more moved in. Most church records do not specify whether a new member was accepted by letter of transfer or as a result of conversion in Rochester. Wage-earning church members moved more often than their business-owning brethren, and there is a strong possibility that the workingman's revival was no more than a statistical mirage created by in-migrating wage earners. A carpenter, say, could have experienced conversion in his home village, then moved from town to town following jobs and transferring into a church in each new community. If at one point he worked for a few months or a year in Rochester and transferred into one of its churches, his name

TABLE 12. PERCENT OF NEW MALE ADMITTANTS TO ROCHESTER
CHURCHES WHO DO NOT APPEAR IN CITY DIRECTORIES

	year of admission*		
	1825–29	1830–31	1832–38
St. Luke's (N=25, 39, 80)	36	21	41
First Presbyterian (N=48, 80, 104)	42	38	59
Second Presbyterian (N=45, 79, 255)	44	46	57

*Pre-revival figures are limited to the years 1825 to 1829 to ensure an equal mathematical chance of inclusion in the directories, which were published in 1827, 1834, and 1838. Men in the first and third time periods were all admitted to churches within two years of a directory. Those admitted during the Finney revival all joined churches three years before or after the publication of a directory. This slight handicap did not, however, keep them from appearing in those documents more often than members of either of the other two groups—further indication that Finney's audience was made up of the most stable elements of the population.

would appear among the working class "converts." There is sound reason to believe that most of these spurious converts were mobile workingmen, and few were transient lawyers and merchants. That poses a troublesome question: does evidence presented in the text indicate the kinds of persons who experienced religion in Rochester, or only the kinds who moved into that city at succeeding stages of its development?

The question can be answered definitively for the congregations at First and Second Presbyterian Churches. Clerks in those churches recorded the names of incoming members and noted whether they entered by letter of transfer or by profession of faith. Thus in these two congregations we may eliminate effects of migration into Rochester on the statistics of revivals.

Table 13 separates new male admittants to these churches into in-migrants and converts. In-migrants accounted for two-thirds of the new members in the 1820s, and little more than one in five during the revivals. But the distribution of occupations among them varied little over time. Laborers increased among the migrants in the 1820s, reflecting changes in the overall makeup of the work force, but the ratio of white-collar

TABLE 13. OCCUPATIONS OF MEN ENTERING FIRST AND SECOND PRESBYTERIAN CHURCHES BY LETTER OF TRANSFER AND BY PROFESSION OF FAITH, 1815–38 (PERCENTAGES)

	year of admission		
	1815–29	1830–31	1832–38
in-migrants (N=64, 18, 36)			
white collar	44	39	42
skilled manual	48	39	39
unskilled-semiskilled	8	22	19
converts (N=33, 74, 114)			
white collar	64	61	30
skilled manual	33	35	60
unskilled-semiskilled	3	4	10

to blue-collar migrants remained stable throughout the years 1815–38. With these men removed from consideration, patterns derived from less refined data become sharper and much more pronounced. In the 1820s and in Charles Finney's revival, businessmen, professionals, and clerks accounted for more than six in ten male converts. Skilled workmen accounted for little more than one in three. These proportions reversed in the years following 1832. Fully seven in ten converts in the middle and late 1830s worked with their hands.

To sum up: at every point, gaps in church membership records have led to underestimates of the number of workingmen who joined churches in the 1830s. Missing records are concentrated among churches with blue-collar memberships, and the number of these churches multiplied after 1831. Coverage in city directories was prejudiced in favor of the more stable (and therefore in most cases the more comfortable) elements of the community. They omit far more workingmen than proprietors. And were we able to separate converts from those who merely moved into Rochester, the transition from businessman's to workingman's revivalism would become much more pronounced.

Notes

INTRODUCTION

1. Charles M. Robinson, *First Church Chronicles, 1815–1915* (Rochester, 1915), 16; Session Minutes, Rochester Brick Presbyterian Church, December 1825; H. Richard Niebuhr, *The Kingdom of God in America* (New York, 1937), 55.

2. Notes to this sermon were recorded in the diary of Bradford King, King Family Papers, University of Rochester, entry for November 28, 1830.

3. Charles G. Finney, *Autobiography of Charles G. Finney* (New York, 1876), 301. Estimates of national church membership are from Winthrop R. Hudson, *Religion in America: An Historical Account of the Development of American Religious Life* (New York, 1973), 128–30; Frank H. Littell, *From State Church to Pluralism: A Protestant Interpretation of Religion in American History* (New York, 1962), 36–39. Works on the revival of 1830–31 are cited in Chapter V, note 34.

4. Perry Miller, *The Life of the Mind in America: From the Revolution to the Civil War* (New York, 1965), 28.

5. Gilbert Hobbs Barnes, *The Anti-Slavery Impulse, 1830–1844* (New York, 1964).

6. The literature on revivalism and reform is immense. For recent surveys, see John L. Thomas, "Romantic Reform in America, 1815–1860," *American Quarterly* 17 (Winter 1965), 656–81; Lois W. Banner, "Religious Benevolence as Social Control: A Critique of an Interpretation," *Journal of American History* 55 (June 1973), 23–41; Ronald G. Walters, *American Reformers, 1815–1860* (New York, 1978).

7. These studies are discussed in the Afterword. For the most thorough of them, see Paul Faler, "Cultural Aspects of the Industrial Revolution: Lynn, Massachusetts Shoemakers and Industrial Morality, 1826–1860," *Labor History* 15 (Summer 1974), 367–94.

8. Bernard Wishy, *The Child and the Republic* (Philadelphia, 1968); Anne L. Kuhn, *The Mother's Role in Childhood Education* (New Haven, 1947).

9. Lee Benson, *The Concept of Jacksonian Democracy: New York as a Test Case* (Princeton, 1961); Ronald P. Formisano, *The Birth of Mass*

Political Parties: Michigan, 1827–1861 (Princeton: 1971); Paul Kleppner, *The Cross of Culture: A Social Analysis of Midwestern Politics* (New York, 1970); Richard Jensen, *The Winning of the Midwest: Social and Political Conflict, 1888–1896* (Chicago, 1971); S. M. Lipset, *Revolution and Counterrevolution: Change and Persistence in Social Structures* (Garden City, 1970), 305–73.

10. Donald G. Mathews, "The Second Great Awakening as an Organizing Process, 1780–1830," *American Quarterly* 21 (Spring 1969), 23–43; T. Scott Miyakawa, *Protestants and Pioneers: Individualism and Conformity on the American Frontier* (Chicago, 1964); and Rowland Berthoff, *An Unsettled People: Social Order and Disorder in American History* (New York, 1971), 235–74, stress migration and social instability as causes of revivals. Status anxieties and/or resentments are major themes of William G. McLoughlin, *Modern Revivalism: Charles Grandison Finney to Billy Graham* (New York, 1959), and Bernard Weisberger, *They Gathered at the River: The Story of the Great Revivalists and Their Impact upon Religion in America* (Boston, 1958). The most perceptive and imaginative recent studies have centered on the problems of youthful self-definition. See Joseph F. Kett, "Growing Up in Rural New England, 1800–1840," in Tamara A. Hareven, ed., *Anonymous Americans: Explorations in Nineteenth-Century Social History* (Englewood Cliffs, N.J., 1971), 1–16; Joseph F. Kett, "Adolescence and Youth in Nineteenth-Century America," in Theodore K. Rabb and Robert I. Rotberg, eds., *The Family in History: Interdisciplinary Essays* (New York, 1971), 95–110; Nancy F. Cott, "Young Women in the Second Great Awakening," *Feminist Studies* 3 (Fall 1975); and Lois W. Banner, "Religion and Reform in the Early Republic: The Role of Youth," *American Quarterly* 23 (December 1971), 677–95. Writing from within the Protestant tradition, church historians look to the disestablishment of state churches and the ensuing theological and organizational accommodation to popular democratic ideas. See Winthrop R. Hudson, *The Great Tradition of the American Churches* (New York, 1953); Sydney E. Mead, *The Lively Experiment: The Shaping of Christianity in America* (New York, 1963); and Littell, *From State Church to Pluralism*.

11. Here I refer to the gap that exists between the intensive social and demographic studies of seventeenth- and eighteenth-century communities and the systematic studies of industrial populations that begin in 1850.

12. The following is based on Durkheim's original formulation, particularly as it has been restated by Thomas Luckmann and Guy

E. Swanson. See Durkheim, *The Elementary Forms of the Religious Life* (New York, 1915); Swanson, *The Birth of the Gods: The Origin of Primitive Beliefs* (Ann Arbor, 1960); Luckmann, *The Invisible Religion: The Problem of Religion in Modern Society* (New York, 1967). The discussion presented here does not do justice to the complexity of any of these arguments, but is a lowest-common-denominator synthesis of the three.

13. Emile Durkheim, *The Rules of Sociological Method* (New York, 1938), 1–2 and *passim*.

14. My discussion of marriage leans heavily upon Swanson, *Birth of the Gods*, 22ff, and Peter L. Berger and Hansfried Kellner, "Marriage and the Construction of Reality," *Diogenes* 46 (1964).

15. This potential has been realized most fully by American historians of France. See especially Charles Tilly, *The Vendée* (Cambridge, 1964), and William H. Sewell, Jr., "Social Change and the Rise of Working-Class Politics in Nineteenth-Century Marseille," *Past and Present* 65 (1974), 75–109.

16. My work has been made much easier by the existence of thorough studies of Rochester and its hinterland during these years. See Blake McKelvey, *Rochester: The Water-Power City, 1812–1854* (Cambridge, 1945), and Whitney R. Cross, *The Burned-Over District: A Social and Intellectual History of Enthusiastic Religion in Western New York, 1800–1850* (Ithaca, 1950).

1 ECONOMY

1. Finney, *Autobiography*, 286–87. The following description of downtown Rochester is taken from Blake McKelvey, "The Physical Growth of Rochester," *Rochester History* 13 (October 1951), 1–24, and from Dorothy S. Truesdale, ed., "American Travel Accounts of Early Rochester," *Rochester History* 16 (April 1954), 1–24.

2. The urban population had grown faster than the rural population between 1790 and 1810, but this was an artificial "windfall" urbanization created by American neutrality, and hence the expansion of the maritime economy, during the Napoleonic Wars. It was concentrated in a few northeastern seaports, and it stopped abruptly when the United States entered the war. Urbanization after 1820 was concentrated in inland marketing and manufacturing cities, and it was tied directly to the commercialization of northern agriculture. See Adna Ferrin Weber, *The Growth of Cities in the Nineteenth Century: A Study in Statistics* (New York, 1899), 23–25; J. G. Williamson, "An-

tebellum Urbanization in the American North and East," *Journal of Economic History* 35 (December 1965), 592–608; George Rogers Taylor, "American Urban Growth Preceding the Railway Age," *Journal of Economic History* 37 (September 1967), 309–39; Cross, *Burned-Over District,* 55–76. Even the old seaports owed most of their growth after 1815 to the commercialization of agriculture. See, for instance, Diane Lindstrom, *Economic Change in the Philadelphia Region, 1810–1850* (New York, 1977).

3. The history of the Genesee Valley in the late eighteenth and early nineteenth centuries can be followed in Anthony F. C. Wallace, *The Death and Rebirth of the Seneca* (New York, 1969); Orasmus Turner, *History of the Pioneer Settlement of Phelps and Gorham's Purchase, and Morris' Preserve* (Rochester, 1851); Neil Adams McNall, *An Agricultural History of the Genesee Valley, 1790–1860* (Philadelphia, 1952).

4. McNall, *Genesee Valley,* 1–70.

5. Blake McKelvey, "The Port of Rochester: A History of Its Lake Trade," *Rochester History* 16 (October 1954), 1–7.

6. McNall, *Genesee Valley,* 109, 248–53. In 1840 Monroe County (Rochester was county seat) was western New York's leading producer of wheat, corn, rye, barley, potatoes, dairy products, hogs, and horses.

7. Henry O'Reilley, *Settlement of the West: Sketches of Rochester* (Rochester, 1838), 362; Whitney R. Cross, "Creating a City: The History of Rochester from 1824 to 1834" (M.A. thesis, University of Rochester, 1936), 323. Almost all of this flour was milled from local wheat. See McNall, *Genesee Valley,* 124, and Douglas C. North, *The Economic Growth of the United States, 1790–1860* (New York, 1966), 105–6.

8. *Directory of the Village of Rochester* (Rochester, 1827), 118–20; *Rochester Daily Democrat,* December 23, 1831.

9. William L. Stone, cited in Truesdale, "Travel Accounts," 19. See also Charles B. Kuhlmann, "The Processing of Agricultural Products in the Pre-Railway Age," in Harold F. Williamson, ed., *The Growth of the American Economy* (New York, 1944), 162–63.

10. H. G. Spafford, *Gazetteer of the State of New York* (New York, 1824), 189–90.

11. *Directory of 1827,* 119; Carl F. Schmidt, *Greek Revival Architecture in the Rochester Area* (Scottsville, N.Y., 1946); O'Reilley, *Settlement of the West,* 372.

12. Harriet A. Weed, comp., *Autobiography of Thurlow Weed* (Boston, 1884), 257.

13. See Kearney's advertisement in the *Directory of the City of Rochester* (Rochester, 1838), 131; these are identified as Catholics in the *Anti-Masonic Enquirer*, September 15, 1829, and James Buchan to Charles Finney, November 16, 1830, Charles Grandison Finney Papers, Oberlin College.

14. Edwin Scrantom Diary, October 24, 1837 (typescript, Rochester Public Library).

15. Patterns of settlement and the values of the settlers are described in Cross, *Burned-Over District*, 3–109; McNall, *Genesee Valley*, 1–77; David Maldwyn Ellis, "The Yankee Invasion of New York," *New York History* 32 (January 1951), 1–17; Dixon Ryan Fox, *Yankees and Yorkers* (New York, 1940); Turner, *Phelps-Gorham Purchase;* and Lois Kimball Mathews, *The Expansion of New England* (New York, 1909).

16. On the Carrolls and Fitzhughs, see Neil Adams McNall, "The Landed Gentry of the Genesee," *New York History* 26 (April 1945), 162–76.

17. On the Rochesters, see Blake McKelvey, "Colonel Nathaniel Rochester," *Rochester History* 24 (January 1962), 1–23; the collection of family materials in Rochester Historical Society *Publications* 3 (1924); and "The Autobiography of Nathaniel Rochester," RHS *Publications* 1 (1922), 53–55.

18. Anson Colman to Catherine Rochester Colman, July 7, 1825, RHS *Publications* 21 (1943), 17.

19. On the Browns and Mumfords, see Turner, *Phelps-Gorham Purchase*, 593–94.

20. Negotiations leading to the purchase can be followed in a published exchange of letters, *Moses Atwater of Canandaigua, N.Y. to Samuel J. Andrews of Derby, Conn. A Packet of Letters Relating to the Early History of Rochester, 1812–1814* (Rochester, 1914). Reminiscences of the Andrews family were published in the *Rochester Daily Democrat*, April 11, 1945.

21. Information on the Stones is from the *Rochester Daily Advertiser*, October 6, 1847, and the *New England Historical and Genealogical Register* 15 (1861), 304.

22. Here we may recall that 59 percent of the 1827 elite had lived in villages that were within fifty miles of Rochester. While each of the proprietors of 1815 maintained networks of kin and associates in the hinterland, only three of the ten (Nathaniel Rochester, Charles Carroll, and William Mumford) had actually lived there. That twice the proportion of the 1827 elite were former residents of the valley

suggests that ties with the countryside thickened as the boom progressed.

23. Bernard Farber, *Guardians of Virtue: Salem Families in 1800* (New York, 1972), 84.

24. Statements here and in the following paragraph pertain to family partnerships among overseas merchants in Salem in 1810, and among the richest 10 percent of property holders in Rochester in 1827, expressed here as percentages:

	Salem (N = 52)	Rochester (N = 34)
relation of the youngest to the oldest partner:		
brother	35	38
brother-in-law	10	29
cousin	8	–
son	29	21
nephew	15	9
son-in-law	4	3

SOURCES: Farber, *Guardians of Virtue*, 85; Rochester partnerships were compiled from the 1827 tax list, from newspaper advertisements, from announcements of the formation and dissolution of partnerships in the Index to Rochester Newspapers (Rochester Public Library), and from biographical data scattered throughout the *Publications* of the Rochester Historical Society. The figures exclude ten Salem partnerships and four Rochester partnerships for which relationships could not be ascertained.

25. Farber, *Guardians of Virtue*, 86. My thinking here has been influenced by Farber and by Peter Dobkin Hall, "Marital Selection in Massachusetts Merchant Families, 1700–1900," in Rose L. Coser, ed., *The Family: Its Structure and Functions* (2nd ed., New York, 1974), 226–39.

26. Among the 42 elite members whose birth dates were ascertained, the median age in 1827 was 36 years.

27. See especially Kenneth Lockridge, "Land, Population, and the Evolution of New England Society," *Past and Present* 39 (1968), 62–80; Philip J. Greven, Jr., *Four Generations: Population, Land, and Family in Colonial Andover, Massachusetts* (Ithaca, 1970); Daniel Scott Smith, "Population, Family, and Society in Hingham, Massachusetts, 1635–1880 (Ph.D. dissertation, University of California,

1973); Robert Gross, *The Minutemen and Their World* (New York, 1976); James Henretta, "Families and Farms: *Mentalité* in Pre-Industrial America," *William and Mary Quarterly* 35 (January 1978), 3–32.

28. On Bissell, the Elys, Hill, and Leavitt, see the biographical sketches in Mary Moulthrop, comp., Copies of Genealogical Data for Monroe County and Adjacent Areas, University of Rochester. On Peck and Andrews, see RHS *Publications* 9 (1932), 296n, and their advertisement in the *Rochester Telegraph*, January 2, 1821.

29. McKelvey, *Rochester*, 167, 213; Henrietta Bissell to Theodore Dwight Weld, August 1, 1831, Theodore Dwight Weld Papers, University of Michigan.

30. They were Frederick Whittlesey, whose family had been among the purchasers of the Andrews-Atwater Tract; Jonothan Child, son-in-law of Nathaniel Rochester; William W. Mumford, son of Thomas Mumford; and Warham Whitney, son-in-law of Samuel J. Andrews.

31. Unless otherwise cited, information on Reynolds is from his "Autobiography," *Rochester Post-Express*, September 23, 1884.

32. Nathaniel Rochester to Nathaniel Thrift Rochester, January 22, 1821, Rochester Family Papers, University of Rochester.

33. *Telegraph*, July 9, 1825.

34. There is a sketch of Kempshall in Turner, *Phelps-Gorham Purchase*, 604–5.

35. See William Stone's description of this mill in Truesdale, "American Travel Accounts," 10.

36. Sponsored mobility and its social implications are discussed in Lawrence Stone, "Social Mobility in England, 1500–1700," *Past and Present* 33 (April 1966), 56–73.

37. Rev. D. W. C. Huntington, "Historical Sermon, Early Rochester Methodists," *Rochester Evening Express*, December 1, 1877, from Blake McKelvey's manuscript notes on Rochester history, cited hereafter as McKelvey Notes. Also McKelvey, *Rochester*, 333n.

38. From the 1830 assessment rolls.

39. Turner, *Phelps-Gorham Purchase*, 605.

40. See the works cited in the Introduction, note 10.

41. The point is made in Thomas Luckmann and Peter L. Berger, "Social Mobility and Personal Identity," *European Journal of Sociology* 5 (1964), 337.

42. For figures on the residential instability of Rochester wage earners, see Chapter II, note 3.

43. The median age of men who joined Presbyterian churches by profession of faith in 1830–31 and whose birth dates were ascertained (N=63) was thirty years. The maturity of the Rochester converts poses a serious problem for the widely held belief that the Second Great Awakening centered among children and youth. Of 131 male converts in the years 1815–38 for whom birth dates are known, only seven experienced conversion before the age of twenty. Of 108 female converts, only five were teenagers. The Rochester revival, obviously, had little to do with the problems of adolescence and youth, and I do not consider that surprising. The works cited in note 27 make it abundantly clear that New England boys had been forced to separate from their parents and to define themselves through their own actions for nearly a hundred years. Certainly the problems of increased autonomy, particularly among very young men, could lead to religious crisis. But I suspect that scholars attempting to draw relationships between youthful independence and enthusiastic religion will find that the relationship was stronger in the eighteenth than in the nineteenth century. For fascinating speculations along these lines, see Greven, *Four Generations,* 274ff, and J. M. Bumsted, "Religion, Finance, and Democracy in Massachusetts: The Town of Norton as a Case Study," *Journal of American History* 57 (March 1971), 817–31.

44. The analysis of land speculators and of the 1827 elite make it clear that many Rochester entrepreneurs formed alliances with in-laws and maternal relatives. But these present peculiarly difficult problems of research. It is understandable that historical studies of extended kinship have thus far been limited to relations between fathers and their married sons, or have depended upon the careful tracing of a few examples. Among the more admirable of these are Greven, *Four Generations;* Smith, "Population, Land, and Family"; and Dorothy Crozier, "Kinship and Occupational Succession," *Sociological Review* 13 (1965), 15–43.

45. The literature on spatial mobility and its relation to occupational success is discussed in Stephan Thernstrom and Peter R. Knights, "Men in Motion: Some Data and Speculations about Urban Population Mobility in Nineteenth-Century America," *Journal of Interdisciplinary History* 1 (Autumn 1970), 7–35. Robert E. Beider draws a firm relationship between stability, economic well-

being, and extended family connections in a mid-nineteenth-century town in "Kinship as a Factor in Migration," *Journal of Marriage and the Family* 35 (August 1973), 429–39.

46. See below, Tables 3 and 4.

47. *Rochester Observer*, October 22, 1830, December 12, 1830, March 3, 1831; Diary of Bradford King, entries for December 22, 1830, December 23, 1830, January 2, 1831; Alvah Strong, *Autobiography* (Rochester, n.d.), 32; Cross, *Burned-Over District*, 155–56.

2 SOCIETY

1. For the derivation of these figures, see Appendix A.

2. In 1830, 76 percent of the Rochester population was under thirty. Among those in their twenties, there were 125 males per 100 females; the ratios were 140/100 for those in their thirties, 119/100 for those in their forties. Computed from the manuscript population schedules for Monroe County, New York, Fifth Census of the United States.

3. *Rochester Album*, May 16, 1826. Persistence rates (the percentage remaining in town) for laborers and for journeymen in four sample trades between 1827 and 1834 were as follows:

	N	persistence
shoemaker	111	20
carpenter	275	17
blacksmith	57	19
cooper	60	13
day laborer	408	15

4. Stuart M. Blumin, "Mobility and Change in Antebellum Philadelphia," in Stephan Thernstrom and Richard Sennet, eds., *Nineteenth-Century Cities: Essays in the New Urban History* (New Haven, 1969), 198. Whatever the exact figures, it is clear that Rochester included a much higher proportion of wage earners than did the only contemporary city that has been studied systematically. Appendix A estimates that there were five journeymen for every master craftsman in Rochester in 1827. Working with a similar method and making similar assumptions, Thomas

Smith estimates that there were approximately equal proportions of journeymen and masters in Philadelphia in 1810. See Thomas L. Smith, "Reconstructing Occupational Structures: The Case of the Ambiguous Artisan," *Historical Methods Newsletter* 8 (June 1975), 134–46.

5. *Telegraph*, January 1, 1821 (advertisement of Jacob Gould). For an overview, see Blake McKelvey, "A History of the Rochester Shoe Industry," *Rochester History* 15 (April 1953), 1–28.

6. Jesse W. Hatch, "The Old-Time Shoemaker and Shoemaking," RHS *Publications* 5 (1926), 81, 83.

7. Hatch, "Shoemaking," 84. This system seems to have been common outside New England between the breakdown of the craft system and the organization of machine industry. See Sam Bass Warner, Jr., *The Private City: Philadelphia in Three Periods of Its Growth* (Philadelphia, 1968), 68–69; Victor S. Clark, *History of Manufactures in the United States* (New York, 1929), 1:444.

8. Brown, Ely, and Tucker are identified as owners of coopers' shops in the 1830 tax list. On the Kings, see their advertisement in the *Monroe Republican*, January 3, 1826.

9. Darrow identified himself as a lumber merchant on the "Petition of Inhabitants of Rochester, N. York to Stop Sunday Mails," dated December 5, 1828, Legislative and Judicial Records Branch, National Archives.

10. Cross, "Creating a City," 104.

11. Elisha Ely, comp., *Rochester in 1827* (Rochester, 1828), 138.

12. *Rochester Observer*, June 6, 1828; *A Directory for the Village of Rochester* (Rochester, 1827), 118.

13. See the advertisements of Derick Sibley (merchant), *Observer*, October 27, 1827; Charles Perkins (lawyer), *Rochester Daily Advertiser*, April 9, 1833; A. B. Buckland (merchant) *Rochester Daily Democrat*, January 9, 1837; Edward R. Everest (shoe dealer), *Daily Democrat*, January 3, 1835. Nathaniel Rochester's building activities are discussed in McKelvey, "Physical Growth of Rochester," 4. There are useful discussions of effects of rapid urbanization on house building and house builders in Daniel J. Boorstin, *The Americans: The National Experience* (New York, 1965), 148–51, and Sam Bass Warner, Jr., *The Urban Wilderness: A History of the American City* (New York, 1972), 66–67, 74.

14. Merchant capitalism was first described by John R. Commons, "American Shoemakers, 1648–1895," *Quarterly Journal of Economics* 24

(1909), 39–84. For more recent discussions, see George Rogers Taylor, *The Transportation Revolution, 1815–1860* (New York, 1968), and Alan Dawley, *Class and Community: The Industrial Revolution in Lynn* (Cambridge, 1976), esp. 11–32.

15. In the 1834 directory (but not in the directory published seven years earlier) many proprietors in these trades were identified as hat dealers, merchant-tailors, and so on.

16. Catherine Josephine Dowling, "Dublin," RHS *Publications* 2 (1923), 241–42. The celebration of St. Monday seems to have been particularly strong and long-lived among coopers. See E. P. Thompson, "Time, Work Discipline, and Industrial Capitalism," *Past and Present* 38 (September 1967), 74–79; Herbert G. Gutman, *Work, Culture, and Society in Industrializing America* (New York, 1974), 37–38.

17. Hatch, "Shoemaking," 82–83.

18. *Daily Democrat*, April 4, 1834.

19. *Observer*, August 8, 1829.

20. *Daily Democrat*, April 15, 1834.

21. For examples, see Alvah Strong, *Autobiography of Alvah Strong* (Rochester, n.d.), 31–32; Hamlet Scrantom to Abraham Scrantom, December 2, 1813 and summer 1820, Hamlet Scrantom Letters, 1812–20, Freeman Clarke Allen Papers, University of Rochester.

22. Chloe Peck to Samuel Porter, December 23, 1820, Porter Family Papers, University of Rochester. Throughout these years the word family was applied to everyone who lived under the same roof. Some examples: "We have quite a large family—seven and sometimes eight in number," Charlotte Blackwell to John W. Claghorn, April 19, 1820, RHS *Publications* 21 (1943), 13; "Our family is pretty large this winter. We have Eliza, Lucy, Maria, Edward, Rebecca & Ely beside your brother and myself, three of these you are acquainted with," Mrs. Sherman Clark, comp., Diaries and Letters of Mrs. Esther Maria Ward Chapin, 1815–1823 (typescript, Rochester Public Library), letter dated January 30, 1821; "We have an addition to our family. A precious charge, 2 fine boys one of eight and the other 10 years of age," Catherine A. Ely to Lydia Finney, June 20, 1832, Finney Papers. For a discussion of this vocabulary at an earlier date, see Philip J. Greven, Jr., "The average size of families and households in the Province of Massachusetts in 1764 and in the United States in 1790: an overview," in Peter Laslett and Richard Wall, eds., *Household and Family in Past Time* (London, 1972), 545–60.

23. Everard Peck to Samuel Porter, April 26, 1821, Porter Papers.

24. Edmund S. Morgan, *The Puritan Family: Religion and Domestic Relations in Seventeenth-Century New England* (New York, 1966), and John Demos, *A Little Commonwealth: Family Life in Plymouth Colony* (New York, 1971) describe the ideology and operations of family government in the seventeenth century. Its persistence into the early nineteenth century is a major theme of Farber, *Guardians of Virtue.*

25. *Telegraph,* February 13, 1825.

26. Robinson, *First Church Chronicles,* 18; Session Minutes, Brick Presbyterian Church, December 1825.

27. Edwin Scrantom, "Old Citizen's Letters," Letter No. 144. (scrapbook, Rochester Public Library).

28. *Observer,* February 8, 1828.

29. *Observer,* March 14, 1828; *Republican,* September 13, 1831.

30. Of those who headed households in 1827, 26 percent of journeymen, 30 percent of laborers, and 24 percent of shopkeepers took in lodgers. The comparable figures for businessmen and professionals and master craftsmen were 14 percent and 8 percent, respectively. For the means by which men were classified as lodgers or co-resident employees, see Appendix A, note to Table 8.

31. The figures are based on a sample of 544 men which includes every wage earner in the following trades: carpenters, coopers, blacksmiths, shoemakers; and a composite group of smaller trades which includes gunsmiths, lastmakers, printers, sashmakers, and tinners. Within the sample, living arrangements varied significantly. Old residential patterns seem to have persisted only where work groups remained small. The figures, broken down by trade, are as follows:

| | householder | | boarder | | |
	owner	renter	private family	boarding-house	employer's home
carpenter (N=275)	17	24	31	11	18
cooper (N=60)	12	28	27	8	25
blacksmith (N=57)	14	26	32	4	25
shoemaker (N=111)	5	29	25	18	23
small-shop trades (N=41)	–	12	29	12	46

For the means by which occupations were derived, see Appendix A.

32. No tax list survives for the years between 1830 and 1837. Thus it is difficult to separate masters from journeymen in 1834. Hatch, "Shoemaking," provides a list of master shoemakers. Masters in the

small-shop trades were identified through newspaper advertisements and scattered references in RHS *Publications*. The addresses of these men in 1834 were then matched with those of others in their trades to produce a figure for co-resident employees. The resulting figures, expressed as percentages, are as follows:

	1827	1834
small-shop craftsman (N=41, 42)		
householder or boarder in private home	42	64
boarder in hotel or boardinghouse	12	7
boarder in employer's household	46	29
shoemakers (N=111, 119)		
householder or boarder in private home	59	59
boarder in hotel or boardinghouse	18	36
boarder in employer's home	23	5

There was a shortage of housing in 1827. It is conceivable that wage earners lived with employers in that year only because they had nowhere else to go, and that they moved out as soon as other housing became available. I doubt, however, that this explains the figures presented here. For if co-residence of master and journeyman was in fact due only to a housing shortage, then we would expect a rise in the proportion of journeymen who owned homes as those homes became available. But that proportion actually declined from 12 percent to 9 percent between 1827 and 1837. The transformation was due not to an increase in home ownership among wage earners but to the fact that workmen were leaving the homes of their employers and entering boardinghouses and households headed by men of their own class.

33. Scrantom, "Old Citizen's Letters," Letter No. 80.

34. For examples, see Strong, *Autobiography*, 31–32; Reynolds, "Autobiography"; and Hatch, "Shoemaking," 81.

35. *Rochester Gem*, March 5, 1831.

36. Unless otherwise cited, this and other descriptions of the downtown area are from scattered references in McKelvey, *Rochester*. Most of them are reiterated in McKelvey, "The Physical Growth of Rochester."

37. The samples include all businessmen, professionals, and master craftsmen in the 1827 tax list and directory, and those listed in the 1834 directory who owned sufficient property in 1830 and/or 1837 to be ranked as proprietors. Laborers include everyone listed with that occupation in 1827 and 1834. Journeymen are

the shoemakers and small-shop craftsmen discussed in note 32. The resulting figures on occupation and residence, expressed as percentages, are as follows:

	1827	1834
businessman-professional (N = 144, 184)		
central business district	44	16
middle-class residential street	14	42
mixed residential street	34	30
working-class residential street	8	11
master craftsman-manufacturer (N = 179, 167)		
central business district	31	14
middle-class residential street	15	36
mixed residential street	40	34
working-class residential street	14	16
journeyman craftsman (N = 110, 152)		
central business district	32	10
middle-class residential street	6	9
mixed residential street	40	34
working-class residential street	30	49
day laborer (N = 338, 349)		
central business district	29	4
middle-class residential street	1	4
mixed residential street	21	21
working-class residential street	49	71

38. The drawing is reproduced in McKelvey, *Rochester,* facing 145. Hall stayed at the Eagle Tavern, and his sketch was clearly done from above ground level, probably from his window.

39. *Directory of 1827;* "Minutes of the Trustees of the Village of Rochester," July 1827 (typescript, Rochester Public Library); Cross, "Creating a City," 248–49.

40. *Daily Democrat,* February 17, 1834.

41. For the emergence of similar patterns in other cities during these years, see Warner, *Private City,* chs. 3–4; Peter R. Knights, *The Plain People of Boston, 1830–1860: A Study in City Growth* (New York, 1971), ch. 4; Allen R. Pred, "Manufacturing in the American Mercantile City, 1800–1840," *Annals of the Association of American Geographers* 56 (1966), 307–38; Stuart M. Blumin, *The Urban Threshold: Growth and Change in a Nineteenth-Century Community* (Chicago, 1975), 104–25; Edward M. Pessen, *Riches, Class, and Power before the Civil War* (Lexington, Mass., 1974), 169–204.

42. Dowling, "Dublin," 233–49; George H. Humphries, "Old East

Avenue Days," RHS *Publications* 6 (1927), 245–53. There is an engraving of the tannery in O'Reilley, *Settlement of the West,* facing 372.

43. *Observer,* September 5, 1828, December 17, 1830. On the development of South Fitzhugh and the surrounding streets, see Charles F. Pond, "History of the Third Ward," RHS *Publications* 1 (1922), 71–81; Carl F. Schmidt, "The Post-Colonial Architecture in Rochester" (typescript, Rochester Public Library); Cross, "Creating a City," 254–55.

44. *Album,* December 22, 1829.

45. Blake McKelvey, "Rochester and the Erie Canal," *Rochester History* 11 (July 1949), 10–11.

46. *Niles Weekly Register* 31 (October 7, 1826), cited in Ronald E. Shaw, *Erie Water West: A History of the Erie Canal, 1792–1854* (Lexington, Ky., 1966)., 231.

47. *Observer,* January 11, 1828. On the audiences, see George M. Elwood, "Some Earlier Public Amusements in Rochester," RHS *Publications* 1 (1922), 17–52.

48. References to the drinking problem are rare in Rochester newspapers until the founding of the *Rochester Observer* in 1827. That paper talked about little else, and its concerns were shared by others. Whitney Cross estimates that after 1827 fully 10 percent of Rochester newspaper space (including advertising) was given over to discussions of temperance (Cross, "Creating a City," 143).

49. *Anti-Masonic Enquirer,* September 15, 1829. According to a study made by Samuel Chipman of Third Presbyterian Church, 70 percent of the inmates at the Rochester poorhouse in 1834 were drunkards or members of the families of drunkards. Another 16 percent, most of them children, were in a doubtful condition. At the jail it was worse. A full 88 percent of the prisoners were alcoholics and all the others, in Chipman's pious estimation, may have been so. When he brought this information before justices of the peace, they agreed that "of the number of criminals brought before us for trial, 7–10 were in a state of intoxication when before us, or when the crime was committed." Samuel Chipman, *Report of an Examination of Poor-Houses, Jails, &c., in the State of New York, and in the Counties of Berkshire, Massachusetts; Litchfield, Connecticut; and Bennington, Vermont* (Albany, 1834), 37, 38.

50. Scrantom, "Old Citizen's Letters," Letters No. 43, 44.

51. Strong, *Autobiography,* 24.

52. Scrantom, "Old Citizen's Letters," Letter No. 4.

53. The temperance movement among proprietors is discussed in Chapter IV.

54. The most recent full-length study of the temperance movement places the development of bourgeois domesticity at its center. See Norman H. Clark, *Deliver Us from Evil: An Interpretation of American Probition* (New York, 1976). For examples from Rochester editorials, see the *Observer*, February 8, 1828, October 9, 1829, September 5, 1828; *Rochester Gem*, December 17, 1831. On the interior of middle-class households during these years, the best study is Nancy F. Cott, *The Bonds of Womanhood: "Woman's Sphere" in New England, 1780–1830* (New Haven, 1977).

55. These and subsequent figures and examples concerning grocery licensees pertain to the 70 persons who obtained licenses in 1827 and who appeared in the directory published that year. They were identified from the "Minutes of the Trustees."

56. Shopkeepers were persons listed with nonclerical white-collar occupations who ranked below the third decile. For a full explanation, see Appendix A. For these figures tavernkeepers, hotelkeepers, and boardinghouse operators have been eliminated from consideration.

57. The discussion of the Stevens bakery is based on inferences from his occupation, the location and structure of his household and of neighboring households and business establishments, and the fact that he was granted a grocery license in 1827.

58. *Observer*, December 17, 1830; *Republican*, April 18, 1830; Dowling, "Dublin," 243.

59. *Republican*, October 31, 1831; *Observer*, December 31, 1830; *Anti-Masonic Enquirer*, September 17, 1833.

60. *Liberal Advocate*, March 3, 1832.

3 POLITICS

1. Still the only full political history of the Antimasons is Charles McCarthy, "The Anti-Masonic Party: A Study of Political Anti-Masonry in the United States, 1827–1840," American Historical Association *Annual Report* for 1902 (Washington, 1903), vol. 1. See also Benson, *The Concept of Jacksonian Democracy*, 11–46; Formisano, *The Birth of Mass Political Parties*, 56–80 and *passim;* Cross, *Burned-Over District*, 113–25; David Brion Davis, "Some Themes of Counter-Subversion: An Analysis of Anti-Masonic, Anti-Catholic, and Anti-Mormon Literature," *Mississippi Valley Historical Review* 47 (September

1960), 205–24; Seymour Martin Lipset and Earl Raab, *The Politics of Unreason: Right-Wing Extremism in America, 1790–1970* (New York, 1970), 34–47.

2. Nathaniel Rochester to Matthew Brown, Jr., May 9, 1817, cited in McKelvey, *Rochester*, 58.

3. On the Bucktail-Clintonian controversy in New York politics, the best introduction remains Dixon Ryan Fox, *The Decline of Aristocracy in the Politics of New York, 1801–1840* (New York, 1919). See also Alvin W. Kass, *Politics in New York State, 1800–1830* (Syracuse, 1965).

4. Howard L. Osgood, "The Struggle for Monroe County," RHS *Publications* 3 (1924), 127–36.

5. There is a full narrative of the bank controversy in McKelvey, *Rochester*, 75–82.

6. The reference to Bucktails as the "merchant party" is from McKelvey, *Rochester*, 57–58. The following are the occupations and religious affiliations of Bucktail and Clintonian leaders, expressed here as percentages:

	Bucktails (N=18)	Clintonians (N=22)
occupation in 1827		
businessman-professional	72	45
master craftsman	6	36
shopkeeper-petty proprietor	11	9
clerical employee	11	9
journeyman craftsman	–	–
laborer-semiskilled	–	–
richest 10 percent of taxpayers	39	36
religious affiliation		
Presbyterian	11	33
Episcopalian	50	19
Methodist	6	–
Baptist	–	–
non-church member	33	48

sources: For Bucktails, "Petition for the Removal of the Utica Bank in Canandaigua Branch to Rochester, Jan. 10, 1822," Rochester Public Library; for Clintonians, Henrietta A. Weed, comp., *Autobiography of Thurlow Weed* (Boston, 1884), 158–59.

7. See "Descendants of Colonel Nathaniel Rochester," RHS *Publications* 3 (1924), 341–67.

8. Robinson, *First Church Chronicles*, 1–23. Competition between these churches included a pamphlet war between the ministers. See Joseph Penney, *Sermon Preached at the Opening of the New Presbyterian Church in Rochester, October 28, 1824* (Rochester, 1824); Francis H. Cuming, *A Note Addressed to the Rev. Joseph Penney, Pastor of the Presbyterian Congregation of Rochester, occasioned by the note appended to the Sermon preached by him at the opening of the New Presbyterian Church in Rochester, October 28, 1824* (Rochester, 1824); and the references to "zealous sectarians" in Cuming, *The Means by which the Prosperity of the Church May Be Promoted; A Sermon, Delivered in St. Luke's Church, Rochester, May 11, 1823* (Rochester, 1824).

9. Charles Carroll to Nathaniel Rochester, November 9, 1817, RHS *Publications* 21 (1943), 10.

10. Nathaniel Rochester to Alanson Douglas, May 11, 1824, RHS *Publications* 21 (1943), 17.

11. Weed, *Autobiography*, 215ff, and Robert Daniel Burns, "The Abduction of William Morgan," RHS *Publications* 6 (1927), 219–30.

12. For a thoughtful and meticulous analysis of the early stages of the movement, see Ronald P. Formisano and Kathleen Smith Kutolowski, "Antimasonry and Masonry: The Genesis of Protest, 1826–1827," *American Quarterly* 29 (Summer 1977), 139–65.

13. Shaw, *Erie Water West*, 129.

14. Ashley Samson Scrapbook, 51:2, McKelvey Notes. See also Formisano and Kutolowski, "Antimasonry and Masonry," 143.

15. *Proceedings of a Convention of Delegates Opposed to Free Masonry, Which Met at Leroy, Genesee Co., N.Y., March 6, 1828* (Rochester, 1828), 7. Cited hereafter as *Antimasonic Proceedings*.

16. Thurlow Weed Barnes, comp., *Memoir of Thurlow Weed* (Boston, 1884), 300–301. Formisano and Kutolowski, "Antimasonry and Masonry," document the formidable power of Masons throughout western New York.

17. *Rochester Daily Advertiser*, February 19, 1828.

18. On Elwood, see RHS *Publications* 13 (1934), 328. Masons are listed in John B. Mullan, "Early Masonic History in Rochester," RHS *Publications* 7 (1928), 7–21. Figures were created by linking these with the eighteen Bucktails who signed the "Petition for the Removal of the Utica Bank in Canandaigua Branch to Rochester, Jan. 10, 1822," Rochester Public Library; and the twenty-two People's Party Activists listed in Weed, *Autobiography*, 158–59. Inclusion is limited to those who appear in the 1827 directory, and who

were thus in Rochester while the Antimasonic controversy was going on.

19. *Antimasonic Proceedings*, 10.

20. Weed's handbill was printed in the *Rochester Daily Telegraph*, October 13, 1828.

21. Of the eighteen Bucktail leaders present in Rochester in 1827, four became Democratic leaders and one became an Antimason. Of the twenty-two Clintonians, only Jacob Gould (who had competed with Thurlow Weed for a nomination in 1824) became a Democrat, and eight became Antimasonic leaders. All of the others disappeared from lists of party activists.

22. "A Brief Sketch of the Life of Nathaniel Rochester, Written by Himself for the Information of His Children," RHS *Publications* 3 (1924), 311.

23. Anson Colman to Catherine Rochester Colman, July 9, 1825, RHS *Publications* 21 (1943), 20.

24. W. Earl Weller, "The Development of the Charter of the City of Rochester, 1817–1938" (M.A. thesis, University of Rochester, 1938), 13–24.

25. See Table 7 in Appendix A.

26. "Minutes of the Trustees," October 19, 1822.

27. *Telegraph*, February 18, 1824.

28. "Minutes of the Trustees," May 16, 1825.

29. The charter was printed in *A Directory of the Village of Rochester* (Rochester, 1827). See also Weller, "Charter of Rochester," 25ff.

30. *Album*, April 11, 1826.

31. Although the decline of these families accelerated after 1828, their withdrawal clearly preceded the Antimasonic excitement. They held only three of the ten trusteeships in 1826 and 1827. See William F. Peck, *History of Rochester and Monroe County, New York* (New York, 1908), 184–201, for lists of village officers.

32. Weller, "Charter of Rochester," 25.

33. Samson Scrapbook, McKelvey Notes.

34. Weed, *Memoir*, 30–31.

35. *Rochester Craftsman*, September 8, 1829, October 20, 1829; *Rochester Republican*, October 20, 1829; *Anti-Masonic Enquirer*, April 14, 1829.

36. These statements are based on the following figures on persons elected as village trustees under the first and second charters. They are expressed here as percentages:

	first charter	second charter
occupation		
businessman-professional	52	50
master craftsman-manufacturer	33	22
shopkeeper-petty proprietor	14	19
clerical employee	–	8
journeyman craftsman	–	–
laborer-semiskilled	–	–
richest 10 percent of taxpayers	62	42
richest 50 taxpayers in 1827	32	21
linked* to richest 50 taxpayers	29	17
offices held by these	80	38
linked* with Rochester, Brown, Ward, or Strong family connections	50	19
offices held by these	65	18
mean number of terms per trustee	2.0	1.4
percent single-term trustees	48	69

*These are persons linked by blood, marriage, or business partnership.

37. This was particularly true before the village elections of 1830. See the *Republican*, February 16, 1830, March 2, 1830, March 16, 1830, March 23, 1830.

38. Gustavus Clark to Thurlow Weed, April 8, 1827, Thurlow Weed Papers, University of Rochester Library; Henry B. Stanton, *Random Recollections* (New York, 1887), 36.

39. On Samson, see the *Observer*, October 3, 1828, and April 24, 1829; on Gould, *Biography of Jacob Gould* (Rochester, 1867), anonymous pamphlet, Rochester Public Library. Both Gould and Samson signed the "Petition of the Inhabitants of Rochester, N. York to Stop Sunday Mails," dated December 5, 1828, Legislative and Judicial Records Branch, National Archives. Weed, of course, did not.

40. *Enquirer*, October 6, 1829, November 10, 1829, January 19, 1830.

41. Elwood, "Some Earlier Public Amusements in Rochester," 23.

42. Stanton, *Recollections*, 27; Glyndon G. Van Deusen, *Thurlow Weed: Wizard of the Lobby* (Philadelphia, 1952), 35.

43. Statements in this paragraph are based on groups of party candidates and activists gathered from the *Anti-Masonic Enquirer* and the *Rochester Republican*, 1828–1830. They are expressed here as percentages:

	Antimasons (N=84)	Democrats (N=74)
occupation in 1827		
businessman-professional	26	30
master craftsman-manufacturer	26	26
shopkeeper-petty proprietor	10	16
clerical employee	7	14
journeyman craftsman	21	11
laborer-semiskilled	10	4
richest 10 percent of taxpayers	24	22
religious affiliation in 1827		
Presbyterian	11	9
Episcopalian	4	4
Baptist	2	–
Methodist	–	4
Roman Catholic	–	3
churchgoing non-communicant*	29	21
non-churchgo	54	59

*Non-communicants are persons who became church members after 1829. The assumption here is that these attended church regularly before experiencing conversion. Evidence pointing in that direction is presented in Chapter 5.

44. The Catholic population of Rochester was small at this time, but Democrats were already campaigning heavily among them. See the description of (Protestant) Democrats' participation in a St. Patrick's Day celebration in the *Republican*, March 23, 1830.

45. "Minutes of the Trustees," May 18, June 1, July 6, July 8, and July 10, 1826.

46. *Observer*, January 11, 1828.

47. McKelvey, *Rochester*, 179.

48. "Minutes of the Trustees," June 5, 1827.

49. *Ibid.*, September 8, 1829.

50. *Ibid.*, August 29, 1826.

4 IMPASSE

1. *Observer*, August 1, 1828. (Father McNamara was mentioned as a founding member, then disappeared from subsequent lists of activists.) On the national temperance movement, see John Allen Krout, *The Origins of Probibition* (New York, 1925), and Joseph R. Gusfield's brief but penetrating *Symbolic Crusade: Status Politics and the American Temperance Movement* (Urbana, 1963). American historians are in need of a thorough, modern monograph along the lines of Brian Harrison, *Drink and the Victorians: The Temperance Question in England, 1815–1872* (Pittsburgh, 1971).

2. *Observer*, October 31, 1828.

3. Lyman Beecher, *Six Sermons on the Nature, Occasions, Signs, Evils, and Remedy of Intemperance* (Boston, 1828), 64. The *Observer* cited these lectures constantly in 1828 and 1829. For the conversion of a leading Presbyterian to Beecher's principles, see Everard Peck to Samuel Porter, April 22, 1828, Porter Papers.

4. The constitution of the society was printed in the *Observer*, August 1, 1828.

5. Beecher, *Six Sermons*, 66.

6. *Observer*, August 28, 1828. Emphasis in original.

7. *Ibid.*, June 6, 1828. Italics in original.

8. *Ibid.*, September 12, 1828.

9. *Ibid.*, September 18, 1828.

10. *Ibid.*, July 31, 1828. Italics in original.

11. *Ibid.*, March 14, 1828.

12. From the constitution, *ibid.*, August 1, 1828.

13. Cross, "Creating a City," 148. It is difficult to determine per capita consumption, for much of the whiskey was sold to visitors and short-term residents who were not a part of Rochester's "official" population. (If census figures were used as a base, we would have to conclude that the average adult in Rochester drank a fifth-gallon of whiskey daily.) More reliable figures for the United States as a whole suggest that alcohol consumption was at an all-time high in the 1820s. See W. J. Rorabaugh, "Estimated U.S. Alcoholic Beverage Consumption, 1790–1860," *Journal of Studies on Alcohol* 37 (March 1976), 357–64.

14. *Observer*, February 15, 1828.

15. *Ibid.*, January 2, 1829.

16. Alexis de Tocqueville, *Journey to America*, ed. J. P. Mayer (Garden City, 1957), 235. For New England blue laws, see Timothy Dwight, *Travels in New England and New York* (Cambridge, 1969), 4:255–56.

17. *Journal of the Senate and Assembly of the State of New York*, April 19, 1825 (McKelvey Notes). Matthew Brown to Thurlow Weed, February 16, 1825, Weed Papers; E. F. Marshall to Lyman Spalding, March 1, 1825, Lyman Spalding Papers, Cornell University.

18. *Observer*, February 1, 1828.

19. *Ibid.*, March 21, 1828. Italics in original.

20. *Ibid.*, March 14, 1828; Cross, "Creating a City," 95–96.

21. *Ibid.*, December 12, 1828. On the national crusade, see Bertram Wyatt-Brown, "Prelude to Abolitionism: Sabbatarian Politics and the Rise of the Second Party System," *Journal of American History* 63 (September 1971), 316–41.

22. *Observer*, February 8, 1828.

23. *Ibid.*, January 9, 1829.

24. Richard M. Johnson, *Report of the Committee on Post-Offices and Post-Roads of the United States Senate* (January 1829), reprinted in Joseph L. Blau, ed., *Social Theories of Jacksonian Democracy* (Indianapolis, 1954), 274–81.

25. *Observer*, March 13, 1829.

26. "Petition of Inhabitants of Rochester, N. York, to Stop Sunday Mails," dated December 5, 1828. Legislative and Judicial Records Branch, National Archives.

27. For examples, see the *Observer*, November 14, 1828, and June 13, 1828.

28. *Ibid.*, December 12, 1828.

29. *Ibid.*, July 31, 1829, August 29, 1828, September 5, 1829; Cross, "Creating a City," 69–70.

30. For the court cases, see *The Craftsman*, January 26, 1830; *Republican*, June 29, 1830; *Enquirer*, October 20, 1830, and October 27, 1829.

31. The figures from which this statement derives were constructed from lists of officers and candidates of the various organizations. They measure the extent to which the leadership of each group was continuous with the leadership of each of the others (expressed as percentages):

	1	2	3	4	5	6
1. Democrats (N=23)	x	–	4	8	42	39
2. Antimasons (N=32)	–	x	16	28	9	–
3. Temperance Society (N=21)	5	17	x	21	21	15
4. Sabbatarians (N=29)	7	28	21	x	–	12
5. anti-Sabbatarians (N=31)	32	10	19	–	x	21
6. Masonic Lodge (N=34)	21	–	17	10	23	x

Of course many men gave time and energy to one group and supported others with no more than their votes and their moral approval. Thus the figures measure only the relative degree to which these parties and movements shared the same leadership. With that qualification, the groupings outlined in the text become quite clear.

32. *Address of the Freemasons of Monroe County to the Public on Returning their Charter* (Rochester, 1829).

33. For attacks upon Freemasonry from within the churches, see *Rochester Advertiser,* June 6, 1828 (Methodists); *Enquirer,* February 24, 1829 (Presbyterians); *Enquirer,* November 24, 1829 (Baptists). There are complaints of economic sanctions leveled against Masons in *The Craftsman,* April 28, 1829, May 5, 1829, August 11, 1829.

34. The following are the religious affiliations of the leaders discussed in note 31, expressed as percentages:

	Democrats	Anti-Masons	Temperance	Sabbatarians	Anti-Sabbatarians	Masons
Presbyterian	39	50	38	69	16	26
Episcopalian	9	12	19	17	23	24
Methodist	4	–	5	3	3	12
Baptist	–	3	5	3	–	–
non-church member	48	35	33	8	59	38

35. Peck, *Rochester and Monroe County,* 383; Weed, *Autobiography,* 270, 296–97; Formisano and Kutolowski, "Antimasonry and Masonry," 145.

36. *Daily Advertiser,* July 28, 1829.

37. Charles P. McIlvaine, *Rev. Mr. McIlvaine in Answer to the Rev. H. U. Onderdonck* (Philadelphia, 1827), 4, 46. On Johnson and At-

kinson, see F. D. W. Ward, *The Churches of Rochester* (Rochester, 1871), 93.

38. McKelvey, *Rochester*, 132–33.

39. Beecher is cited in Wyatt-Brown, "Prelude to Abolitionism," 331. For examples of Bissell's fund-raising style, see Josiah Bissell to Gerrit Smith, July 10, 1828, and August 12, 1828, Gerrit Smith Papers, Syracuse University.

40. *The Craftsman*, April 9, 1830.

41. Every Protestant congregation in Rochester experienced a rise in new admissions in 1827, then a sharp drop that did not reverse until the Finney revival. Graphs demonstrating this trend are presented in Paul E. Johnson, "A Shopkeeper's Millennium: Society and Revivals in Rochester, New York, 1815–1837" (Ph.D. dissertation, UCLA, 1975), 196–201.

42. J. E. A. Smith, *The History of Pittsfield, Berkshire County, Massachusetts* (Boston, 1876), 2:394.

43. Josiah Bissell to Charles Finney, September 15, 1829, Finney Papers.

5 PENTECOST

1. Robert L. Stanton to Charles Finney, January 12, 1872, Finney Papers.

2. Cross, *Burned-Over District*, 155. The most complete narrative of the Rochester revival is in Robert S. Fletcher, *A History of Oberlin College from Its Founding through the Civil War* (Oberlin, 1943), 1: 17–24.

3. Bradford King Diary, November 11, 1830 (notes to a Finney sermon).

4. Charles G. Finney, *Lectures on Revivals of Religion*, ed. William G. McLoughlin (Cambridge, 1960), 52.

5. Bradford King Diary, November 9, 1830. Finney's published sermons and his *Lectures on Revivals* were attempts to justify his methods and their theological implications to academic seminarians. The plan of salvation as it was understood in the churches was often confused, but tended in the same direction as Finney's more academic formulations. In 1825 the founding congregation at Brick Presbyterian Church in Rochester affirmed their faith that "the only reason why men do not embrace the Gospel is a voluntary opposition to God and holiness. And that the nature of this opposition is such, that none will believe in Christ, but as faith is wrought in their hearts by the

influence of the Holy Ghost." This was pure Finney, but they went on to affirm "that God did from Eternity choose some of our sinful race to everlasting life, through sanctification of the spirit unto obedience and belief of the truth, so that repentence, faith and obedience are not the cause but the effect of election." In the summer following the Finney revival, the trustees threw out these articles and wrote new ones. While reaffirming a strong belief in original sin, they stated that "we believe God, in infinite goodness, has provided a savior for lost man, who is Jesus Christ and that in consequence of his atonement, righteousness, and intercession, all who will repent of their sins and believe in him, will be saved from hell, and received to eternal glory," then reminded themselves that "none can believe until they are renewed by the Holy Ghost." (Brick Church Session Minutes, December 1825 and June 1831).

6. Finney, *Lectures on Revivals*, 125.

7. *Observer*, January 8, 1830.

8. Diary of Nathaniel Thrift Rochester, September 4, 1836 (notes to a sermon), University of Rochester. This lecture was delivered during the revival of 1836, but Whitehouse had been minister to St. Luke's Church since 1829.

9. Finney, *Lectures on Revivals*, 68.

10. Everard Peck to Samuel Porter, January 1, 1831, Porter Papers.

11. Ferdinand D. W. Ward to Henrietta Ward, May 21, 1831, Freeman Clarke Papers, University of Rochester.

12. Melania Smith to Charles Finney, January 10, 1831, Finney Papers.

13. James Buchan to Charles Finney, November 16, 1830, Finney Papers. For further comments on the strategy of family visits, see Cross, *Burned-Over District*, 176.

14. *Observer*, November 12, 1830.

15. Jane Porter to Samuel D. Porter, December 17, 1830; Everard Peck to Samuel Porter, January 11, 1831; S. D. Porter to Samuel Porter, January 31, 1832, Porter Papers.

16. Bradford King Diary, undated account of conversion in October 1830, and entries for December 9, 1830, January 22, 1831, and February 1, 1831. Emphasis in original.

17. Bradford King Diary, December 18, 1830.

18. Finney, *Autobiography*, 291–92.

19. H. Pomeroy Brewster, "The Magic of a Voice: Rochester Revivals of Rev. Charles G. Finney," RHS *Publications* 4 (1925), 281; Robinson, *First Church Chronicles*, 78.

20. *Observer,* October 15, 1830. Every congregation took in large numbers of new members while Finney was in Rochester. It started among Finney's own Presbyterians, but their gains were matched in every church but the Methodist. Initially, Finney came to Rochester at the invitation of Third Presbyterian Church. That congregation added 159 new members between December and March, roughly doubling in size. Baptists, who shared the Presbyterians' New England Calvinist inheritance, also doubled their numbers. But Finney's message transcended cultural and theological traditions. At the end of 1831, vestrymen at St. Luke's counted their total communicants. A full 49.4 percent were new within the preceding year. At First Baptist the comparable figure was a near-identical 50.2 percent. See St. Luke's Church, Parish Register (a year-by-year tabulation of the membership in the 1830s is included at the end of the volume); *Minutes of the Anniversary of the Monroe Baptist Association* (Rochester, annually after 1828); and Rev. Andrew Gillies to Orlo J. Price, October 4, 1932, Local History Division, Rochester Public Library. Similar figures for other churches are unavailable. Their records list incoming members, but fail to name people who either died or left the church. Thus there is no means of determining the year-by-year size of most congregations. For the volume of annual outmigration, see Appendix B, Table 11.

21. Bradford King Diary, October 1830.

22. Finney, *Lectures on Revivals,* 69. Cf. 124–39.

23. The following two paragraphs are pieced together from Finney, *Autobiography,* 288–89; *Observer,* February 17, 1831, and March 3, 1831; Bradford King Diary, December 28, 1830; Stanton, *Random Recollections,* 41–42. On all the new measures, see Cross, *Burned-Over District,* 173–84.

24. Finney, *Autobiography,* 298.

25. *Observer,* November 12, 1830.

26. McKelvey, *Rochester,* 179.

27. My interpretation of these figures may be questioned, for it is not possible to control them for the age of household heads. Of those whose birth dates are known, the median age of Finney's converts was thirty years. It is possible that their households included few employees only because they were beginning in business and did not as yet employ many men. Tax assessments and newspaper advertisements, however, suggest that they operated substantial businesses. More important are the figures in Table 6. If the relative absence of

wage earners in convert-headed households was indeed due to the youth of household heads, then we would expect a relative increase in the number of men in their families as time went on. But they removed men from their homes faster than other (presumably older) entrepreneurs. While the youth of Finney's converts has doubtless distorted the figures in Table 5 (it helps to account for the relative absence of sons over the age of sixteen, for example), I think that the figures on co-residing employees reflect the business practices and social attitudes of Finney's converts, and not their ages.

28. This statement is based on the percentages of women among the new communicants in four congregations in the pre- and post-revival years. These are the only four churches whose records both include women members and span the 1820s and 1830s. Figures for peak revival years are in italics.

	1815–29	1830–31	1832–38
First Presbyterian (N=395, 214, 365)	69.9	*58.9*	69.0
Second Presbyterian (N=150, 218, 619)	60.7	63.8	*54.7*
St. Luke's Episcopal (N=158, 133, 276)	72.2	*66.2*	69.6
St. Paul's Episcopal (N=6, 63, 138)	(50.0)	77.8	*71.7*

Graphs demonstrating the annual numbers of new members in these churches are presented in Johnson, "A Shopkeeper's Millennium," 196–201.

29. *Liberal Advocate*, September 29, 1832. For clerical worries about the role that Finney was assigning to women, see Charles C. Cole, Jr., "The New Lebanon Convention," *New York History* 31 (October 1950), 385–97; Cross, *Burned-Over District*, 177–78.

30. On the creation of a distinct women's sphere among the middle class and the centrality of religion to that sphere, see Cott, *The Bonds of Womanhood;* Mary P. Ryan, "A Woman's Awakening: Revivalistic Religion in Utica, New York, 1800–1835" (unpublished paper, 1976); Ann Douglas Wood, *The Feminization of American Culture* (New York, 1976); Barbara Welter, "The Feminization of American Religion, 1800–1860," in Mary Hartman and Lois W. Banner, eds., *Clio's Consciousness Raised: New Perspectives on the History of Women* (New York, 1974), 137–57; and Carroll Smith Rosenberg, *Religion and the Rise of the American City: The New York City Mission Movement, 1812–1870* (Ithaca, 1971), esp. 97–124.

31. Plotted from the *Observer*, 1830–31.

32. Samuel W. Dike, "A Study of New England Revivals," *American Journal of Sociology* 15 (November 1909), 375.

33. Cited in James A. Hotchkin, *A History of the Purchase and Settlement of Western New York . . . and of the Presbyterian Church in that Section* (New York, 1848), 160.

34. Finney, *Autobiography*, 301. For accounts of the revival of 1831 outside Rochester, see Cross, *Burned-Over District*, 252–54; Roy H. Nichols, *Presbyterianism in New York State: A History of the Synod and its Predecessors* (Philadelphia, 1963), 101–3; Charles R. Keller, *The Second Great Awakening in Connecticut* (New Haven, 1942), 48–49; David M. Ludlum, *Social Ferment in Vermont, 1791–1850* (Montpelier, 1948); Weisberger, *They Gathered at the River*, 130; Dike, "New England Revivals"; and McLoughlin, *Modern Revivalism*, 57.

35. Bradford King Diary, December 18, 1830.

36. Cited in Ernest R. Sandeen, *The Roots of Fundamentalism: British and American Millenarianism, 1800–1930* (Chicago, 1970), 49. My brief discussion of these ideas relies heavily on Niebuhr, *The Kingdom of God in America*, Cross, *Burned-Over District*, and Ernest Lee Tuveson, *Redeemer Nation: The Idea of America's Millennial Role* (Chicago, 1968).

37. Brick Church Session Minutes, December 1825.

38. *Ibid.*, June 1831 (my emphases).

39. William James, *The Debt of Nations to Christianity. A Discourse Delivered in Rochester, June 8, 1828* (Rochester, 1828), 11 and *passim*. Italics in original.

40. Gerald B. F. Hallock, *A Living Church: The First Hundred Years of the Brick Church in Rochester* (Rochester, 1925), 124–25.

41. O'Reilley, *Settlement of the West*, 295. For similar developments in Sunday-school curricula in 1831, see Judith M. Wellman, "The Burned-Over District Revisited: Religion and Reform in Ithaca, Paris, and Mexico, New York" (Ph.D. dissertation, University of Virginia, 1975), esp. 243. That the ideas of individual accountability and moral free agency were central to the revivals of the 1830s has been spelled out most clearly by students of the antislavery movement. See especially Lewis Perry, *Radical Abolitionism: Anarchy and the Government of God in Antislavery Thought* (Ithaca, 1973); and David Brion Davis, "The Emergence of Immediatism in British and American Antislavery Thought," *Mississippi Valley Historical Review* 49 (September 1962), 209–30.

42. William Wisner, *A Narrative of the State of Religion in the Second*

Presbyterian Church in Rochester, Monroe County, N.Y. From the First Sabbath in May, 1831, to the First Sabbath in May, 1833 (Rochester, 1833), 3.

43. *Observer,* February 10, 1831; Mary Gill to Charles Finney, January 18, 1831, Finney Papers; F. D. W. Ward to Henrietta Ward, January 6, 1833, Clarke Papers; Finney, *Lectures on Revivals,* 111; Bradford King Diary, November 28, 1830, and November 13, 1830.

44. Brick Church Session Minutes, September 8, 1833, and September 14, 1833.

45. There is a summary of Weld's lecture in the *Rochester Gem,* April 16, 1831. See also the *Observer,* January 7, 1831.

46. *Observer,* January 13, 1831.

47. Everard Peck to Samuel Porter, January 11, 1831, Porter Papers.

48. *Daily Advertiser,* March 19, 1831.

49. *Observer,* October 29, 1830.

50. *Daily Advertiser,* January 1, 1834.

51. Cross, *Burned-Over District,* 211–14.

52. Brewster, "Magic of a Voice," 281.

6 CHRISTIAN SOLDIERS

1. Levi Parsons, *History of Rochester Presbytery* (Rochester, 1889), 254–56; Hotchkin, *Purchase and Settlement of Western New York,* 491; Price, "One Hundred Years of Protestantism," 250; *Republican,* September 27, 1831. The movement to establish free churches had begun the previous spring in New York City. The first minister to New York's First Free Presbyterian Church was Joel Parker, formerly of Rochester Third Church. See Charles C. Cole, Jr., "The Free Church Movement in New York City," *New York History* 34 (July 1953), 284–97. On Parker, see Dumas Malone, ed., *Dictionary of American Biography* (New York, 1934), 14:231.

2. See the description of the congregation at Bethel Presbyterian in Walter E. Hastings, et al., *A Century with Central Presbyterian Church, 1826–1936* (Rochester, 1936), 4–5.

3. First Methodist Trustees Book, March 19, 1832.

4. *Daily Democrat,* January 8, 1835; Autobiography of Elijah Hebard (manuscript, Rochester Public Library), 84.

5. Marilla Marks, ed., *Memoir of the Life of David Marks, Minister of the Gospel* (Dover, New Hampshire, 1846), 362, 363n.

6. Austin Steward, *Twenty-two Years a Slave, and Forty a Freeman* (Rochester, 1867), 292–98; Cross, "Creating a City," 106.

7. *Republican*, June 21, 1831; *Observer*, July 21, 1831; Cross, "Creating a City," 91–92; Raymond H. Arnot, *The Rochester Savings Bank* (Rochester, 1911).

8. Price, "One Hundred Years of Protestantism," 264; Harry Anstice, *Annals of St. Luke's* (Rochester, 1883), 34; Robinson, *First Church Chronicles*, 79 (quotation).

9. Cross, "Creating a City," 154; O'Reilley, *Settlement of the West*, 306–8.

10. Cross, *Burned-Over District*, 188–89, provides a sketch of Burchard.

11. Mary Mathews to Lydia Finney, February 25, 1832, Finney Papers. The growth of individual congregations is described in Johnson, "Shopkeeper's Millennium," 196–201. For descriptions of these revivals, see F. D. W. Ward to Henrietta Ward, February 21, 1832, Clarke Papers; Wisner, *Narrative of the State of Religion*; G. H. Barnes and D. L. Dumond, eds., *Letters of Theodore Dwight Weld, Angelina Grimke Weld, and Sarah Grimke, 1822–1844* (New York, 1934), 1:40; H. B. Stanton to A. A. Phelps, March 5, 1835, A. A. Phelps Papers, Boston Public Library; Scrantom, "Old Citizen's Letters," Letter No. 123; Cross, "Creating a City," 128–29; Price, "One Hundred Years of Protestantism," 260.

12. The following are the occupations of new male admittants to Rochester Protestant churches in the 1820s and 1830s. Coverage is necessarily limited to persons who appeared in city directories, which results in a significant underestimate of the number of wage earners who joined churches, particularly in the years after 1831. For an indication of the size of this distortion, see Appendix B. The available figures are expressed here as percentages:

	year of admission		
	1825–29 (N=85)	1830–31 (N=170)	1832–38 (N=253)
businessman-professional	22	19	11
shopkeeper-petty proprietor	14	11	13
master craftsman	16	26	16
clerical employee	12	10	8
journeyman craftsman	24	22	41
laborer-semiskilled	13	12	11

13. Available records provide these figures on increases in church membership within occupational groups between 1827 and 1837, presented here as percentages:

	1827	1837	percent change
businessman-professional	32	49	+35
master craftsman-manufacturer	21	62	+66
shopkeeper-petty proprietor	16	23	+30
clerical employee	8	33	+78
journeyman craftsman	3	15	+80
laborer-semiskilled	2	7	+71

The demonstrable increases among wage earners are impressive, but the workingman's revival was very much greater than these figures indicate. For a full discussion of church records and transiency in relation to the revivals of the 1830s, see Appendix B. Peter R. Knights, "City Directories as Aids to Antebellum Urban Studies: A Research Note," *Historical Methods Newsletter* 2 (September 1969), 1–10, discusses coverage in the city directories.

14. Without exception, the churches that took in large numbers of working-class communicants after 1832 were controlled by middle-class laymen. The trustees who invited Burchard into Brick Church included some of the wealthiest merchants and manufacturers in town. Free Presbyterian and Second Baptist were both middle-class missions, controlled by evangelical entrepreneurs throughout the 1830s. The Methodists, who benefited enormously from these revivals, were led by the hat manufacturer Willis Kempshall, the furniture dealer Bill Colby, and the master shoemaker Elihu Grover. The one working-class church that remained free of middle-class control was Reformed Presbyterian, a small congregation of immigrant Scots. For fuller discussions of these churches, see Appendix B.

15. Hatch, "Shoemaking," 82–83.

16. *Daily Advertiser*, April 9, 1833; *Anti-Masonic Enquirer*, April 9, 1833.

17. See *Daily Advertiser*, March 18, 1831, on the boat builders; *Daily Democrat*, April 30, 1835, on the stonemasons; on the continuing organization of journeyman carpenters, see *Daily Democrat*, April 17, 1834, February 2, 1835, and *Republican*, April 19, 1836, and April 26, 1836. See also Cross, "Creating a City," 179–80.

18. The term is from Harrison, *Drink and the Victorians,* 22ff. Evidence of secular self-improvement among workingmen in the 1830s is scattered throughout Bruce Laurie, "Nothing on Compulsion: Life Styles of Philadelphia Artisans, 1820–1860," *Labor History* 15 (Summer 1974), 337–66; David Montgomery, "The Shuttle and the Cross: Weavers and Artisans in the Kensington Riots of 1844," *Journal of Social History* 5 (Summer 1972), 411–46; Faler, "Cultural Aspects of the Industrial Revolution."

19. For a celebration of Paine's birthday, see *Republican,* January 10, 1837. Evidence of active anticlericalism among tramping journeyman shoemakers is in Hatch, "Shoemaking," 82–83. The *Liberal Advocate* (1832–34) and *The World as It Is* (1836) were free-thought papers published in Rochester. There is a discussion of and copious quotations from the former in Joseph W. Barnes, "Obediah Dogberry: Rochester Freethinker," *Rochester History* 36 (July 1974), 1–24. On Painite propriety, see Eric Foner, *Tom Paine and Revolutionary America* (New York, 1976), 47–52, 96–97, and *passim.* See also Albert Post, *Popular Free Thought in America, 1825–1850* (New York, 1943).

20. Jedediah Burchard, for instance, was one of the great spiritual levelers. During a sermon at Brick Church in 1832, Burchard left the pulpit and preached from his knees in front of the mill owner and militia general Ebenezer Beach. Addressing Beach by name, Burchard insisted that he take a public stand for Jesus. The stubborn (and doubtless angry) General Beach persisted in his sins. But the back pews were filled with journeymen and clerks, and the membership records of that church suggest that many of them were glad to come forward and announce their spiritual superiority over Ebenezer Beach and other wealthy but unregenerate men. See Scrantom, "Old Citizen's Letters," Letter No. 123.

21. *The World as It Is,* April 9, 1836.

22. *Daily Democrat,* June 1834, cited in RHS *Publications* 17 (1934), 166.

23. *Daily Advertiser,* March 19, 1831.

24. *Republican,* March 26, 1836.

25. *Observer,* October 15, 1830.

26. *Daily Democrat,* January 9, 1837.

27. The literature on spatial mobility and its relation to economic well-being in nineteenth-century cities is assessed in Thernstrom and Knights, "Men in Motion," and in Thernstrom, *The Other Bostonians: Poverty and Progress in the American Metropolis, 1880–1970* (Cambridge, 1973), 220–61, 9–44.

28. The following figures compare the persistence of non-church

members with that of persons who joined churches in or before 1834:

	N	persistence 1834–38
clerk		
church member in 1834	10	70
non-church member	60	28
journeyman shoemaker		
church member in 1834	12	50
non-church member	101	15
journeyman small-shop craftsman		
church member in 1834	15	60
non-church member	27	11
day laborer		
church member in 1834	13	54
non-church member	330	17
wage earners combined		
church member in 1834	50	58
non-church member	518	16

Of course these figures are suspect, for they do not control for age. Movement from place to place is most common among propertyless young men, and it is likely that church members were older, more secure, and thus more stability-prone than other wage earners. We must attempt to control for that possibility. The ages of household heads are listed in the census of 1830. Tax rolls provide property holdings in that year, and the directory of 1834 lists occupations. Together, these create figures that control for age and occupational status as of 1830. The resulting sample is small and top-heavy. Every man included owned property and headed a household, criteria that eliminate most wage earners at the outset. And each lived in Rochester in 1834, restricting coverage to men who had already persisted for at least four years—again, a small minority of the wage-earning population. To put it simply, the resulting figures on residential persistence are loaded for stability:

	persistence, 1834–1838, by age in 1830		
	20–29	30–39	40+
church member in 1834 (N=6, 17, 13)	50	59	69
non-church member (N=21, 39, 33)	47	41	35
combined (N=21, 39, 33)	48	49	48

The first inference to be made from these figures is that with occupation and home ownership controlled, age had nothing to do with stability. Wage earners in their twenties, thirties, and forties all persisted at the same rate. And with occupation, property holdings, and age controlled, membership in a Protestant church remains a strong predictor of stability. The number of cases is too small to permit confident generalization, but the figures suggest that church members moved often in their twenties and settled down after that. Non-church members kept moving regardless of their age.

Whatever determined a man's willingness or ability to stay in Rochester, it related powerfully to membership in a Protestant church. But the question remains: in what direction did the relationship run? Churches were important community institutions. Admission into one of them constituted a public declaration that a man considered himself a member of the community and that he wished to be considered as such by others. Thus it may have been that churches recruited stability-prone men, and that church membership was more a symptom than a cause of residential persistence. Perhaps that was true in many cases. But home ownership is an equally strong predictor of the intention to stay, and every man in the sample owned his own house. With that crucial variable held constant, churchgoing wage earners persisted at a rate of 61 percent between 1834 and 1838. The comparable figure for non-church members was 40 percent. Without question, membership in a Protestant church was an independent determinant of residential stability.

29. The following three paragraphs are based on an analysis of occupational mobility among churchgoing and non-churchgoing wage earners between 1827 and 1837. Church members included every person who worked for wages in 1827, remained in Rochester in 1837, and joined a church in the intervening years. Non-church members are drawn from large samples rather than the total population. Clerical employees include only clerks; journeymen include carpenters, shoemakers, coopers, blacksmiths, tinners, printers, gunsmiths, lastmakers, and sashmakers; laborers include only laborers. Exclusion of church members in other occupations results in no significant variations from the figures presented here:

occupation in 1827	N	occupation in 1837					
		1	*2*	*3*	*4*	*5*	*6**
clerical employee							
church member	18	61	–	11	28	–	–
non-church member	4	25	–	25	–	50	–
journeyman craftsman							
church member	32	–	53	3	–	41	3
non-church member	23	–	18	4	7	57	14
laborer-semiskilled							
church member	15	13	7	–	–	47	33
non-church member	14	–	–	7	7	29	57

*1 = businessman-professional; 2 = master craftsman-manufacturer; 3 = shopkeeper-petty proprietor; 4 = clerical employee; 5 = journeyman craftsman; 6 = laborer-semiskilled.

30. Parsons boarded with the master carpenter Hezekiah Eldredge in 1827, joined First Presbyterian Church in 1831, and entered into partnership with Eldredge in 1832. See Mary E. Rusk, "Hezekiah Eldredge (1795–1845): Master Builder of Western New York and the Western Reserve" (typescript, Rochester Public Library).

31. Of the proprietors converted during the Finney revival who were in partnership with others, fully 55 percent were in business with relatives.

32. *Republican*, September 27, 1836. Unless otherwise cited, materials on Selye are from a sketch in Mary Moulthrop, comp., Copies of Genealogical Materials for Monroe County and Adjacent Areas, University of Rochester.

33. *Daily Democrat*, February 17, 1834.

34. Edwin Scrantom Diary, May 7, 1838.

35. Strong, *Autobiography*, 1–37. Quotations, 35, 36.

36. Brick Church Session Minutes, undated entry for summer 1834. McKelvey, *Rochester*, 316.

37. Brick Church Session Minutes, October 20, 1832.

38. Elizabeth Eaton to Amos B. Eaton, April 20, 1833, RHS *Publications* 21 (1943), 46.

39. Strong, *Autobiography*, 37–38.

40. The following are figures on party candidates and campaigners between 1834 and 1837, gathered from notices in the *Daily Democrat* and the *Republican*:

	Whigs (N=95)	Democrats (N=76)
occupational group in 1837		
businessman-professional	46	29
master craftsman-manufacturer	27	18
shopkeeper-petty proprietor	12	25
clerical employee	4	9
journeyman craftsman	9	15
laborer-semiskilled	1	4
richest 10 percent of taxpayers	32	19
religious affiliation in 1837		
Presbyterian	25	11
Episcopalian	20	22
Baptist	7	3
Methodist	9	–
Quaker	3	–
Roman Catholic	–	4
non-church member	36	60

The nearly equal proportions of Episcopal Whigs and Democrats hide sharp differences between the two congregations. St. Luke's included sixteen Whig activists and six Democrats. St. Paul's included nine Democrats and only three Whigs. Led throughout these years by the Democrat Elisha Johnson, St. Paul's was the one church in Rochester that did not participate heavily in the Finney revival. It became the home of refugee Democrats, many of them from other denominations. Of those who can be traced to other churches, every member up to 1830 came from the other Episcopal congregation. But after that date there were men in every church who disliked what their congregations were doing. Of sixteen men who entered St. Paul's in the 1830s and whose prior affiliations are known, ten were former Presbyterians and Methodists. At least six of these were among the Democratic Party's leadership cadre. Every other church was a Whig stronghold. St. Paul's, apparently, was the one place in Rochester where churchgoing Democrats could worship in peace.

41. These figures refer to persons who were active in the parties and associations of the late 1820s, and who remained in Rochester in 1834. Whig affiliations are inferred from the petition described in note 54.

	N	percent Whig petitioners		
		church members	*non-church members*	*total*
Bucktails	14	75	0	64
Clintonians	14	80	50	71
Democrats	20	10	10	10
Antimasons	25	83	86	84
temperance advocates	16	82	80	81
Sabbatarians	18	73	–	73
anti-Sabbatarians	18	33	44	39
Masonic Lodge	27	52	33	48

42. McKelvey, *Rochester*, 184–87. The charter was printed in full in *Charter and Directory of the City of Rochester* (Rochester, 1834).

43. "Minutes of the Trustees," May 10, 1832, May 15, 1832, May 22, 1832. The figure of twenty-eight licenses refers to the period May 1832 through May 1833. See also McKelvey, *Rochester*, 179.

44. "Minutes of the Trustees," May 16, 1833.

45. *Anti-Masonic Enquirer*, September 17, 1833. Sixty-eight of the 100 vigilantes later signed the "Memorial of Merchants and Others of Rochester, New York, Praying that Measures of Relief May Be Speedily Adopted," a Whig petition protesting Andrew Jackson's removal of government deposits from the Bank of the United States. U.S. Senate, *Public Documents*, 23d Cong., 1st Sess. (1834), Doc. 349.

46. *Daily Democrat*, April 29, 1834.

47. *Ibid.*, June 11, 1834.

48. *Liberal Advocate*, June 14, 1834.

49. O'Reilley, *Settlement of the West*, 265. To ensure that at least one member of the council would be familiar with the doings of the previous government, the charter provided that the terms of mayors overlap six months with those of aldermen. Child had been appointed by the Whig-temperance aldermen in 1834.

50. *Ibid.*, 266.

51. *Republican*, June 7, 1836.

52. Prominent Democrats, including the Catholic Henry O'Reilley, were among those who signed a plea for funds to establish a reading room for the town's young men, and thus keep them away from "eating houses with each a newspaper and a *bar*—bowling allies with their temptations to betting—gaming tables with their enthralling allurements and degrading companionship—and enticements to

every vicious indulgence . . . dilligently provided by those who excite
appetite and feed passion for the sake of emolument." *Daily Democrat,*
December 1, 1838.

53. *Observer,* December 10, 1830, December 31, 1830, and January
7, 1831.

54. There are, of course, problems with using the bank memorial to identify Whig voters. First, we must assume that the same
men supported the Whigs on both national and local issues: probable, but not provable. More important, there are the one in four

| | N | Whig petitioners | | | |
		church member	*non-church member*	*total*	*est. Whig voters*
occupation in 1830*					
businessman-professional	141	65	38	52	69
master craftsman	133	65	32	53	71
shopkeeper	50	48	30	38	51
home-owning clerk	19	71	25	42	56
home-owning journeyman	110	50	35	41	55
home-owning laborer	52	33	23	25	33
sample proprietors					
mill owner	21	92	67	81	100
lawyer	31	61	38	52	69
doctor	28	73	31	54	72
merchant	63	76	40	52	69
forwarder	18	50	70	61	81
hotel owner	31	0	41	35	47
boardinghouse operator	15	100	7	13	17
grocer	59	83	49	59	79
sample wage earners					
clerk	84	69	26	35	47
journeyman carpenter	209	38	15	23	31
journeyman shoemaker	119	35	9	13	17
journeyman, small shop	44	53	24	39	52
day laborer	340	31	8	10	13

*Includes only men listed in both the 1834 directory and the 1830 tax list.
SOURCE: "Memorial of the Merchants and Others of Rochester, New York,
Praying that Measures of Relief May be Speedily Adopted," U.S. Senate,
Public Documents, 23d Cong., 1st Sess. (1834), Doc. 349.

Whigs who did not sign the petition. It is likely that proprietors had easier access to the petition than did others. The document was in fact labeled a memorial of "Merchants and Others." The fifth column of figures cited above assumes that petitioners represented three-fourths of Whig voters within each occupation. Doubtless that has resulted in an overestimate of Whig support within the business community and an underestimate of Whig strength within the working class. Still, it is clear that Whigs drew their most reliable support from among the members of Protestant churches, regardless of social class. The figures are presented here as percentages.

55. James Gordon Bennett, "Diary of a Trip Through Western New York, 1831" (photocopy, Rochester Public Library). Bennett's parentheses have been deleted.

56. Congregational control is one of the staples of American church history. In terms of the discussion here, a useful statement of the theme is Sidney E. Mead, "The Rise of the Evangelical Conception of the Ministry in America, 1607–1850," in H. Richard Neibuhr and Daniel D. Williams, eds., *The Ministry in Historical Perspectives* (New York, 1956). The statement that a society's dominant religion is determined by the religious needs of its dominant groups underlies nearly everything that Max Weber wrote on the subject of religion. It is most explicit in "The Social Psychology of the World Religions," in Hans Gerth and C. Wright Mills, eds., *From Max Weber: Essays in Sociology* (New York, 1946).

AFTERWORD

1. Alexis de Tocqueville, *Democracy in America*, ed. Phillips Bradley (New York, 1945), 1: 318.

2. Cross, *Burned-Over District*, 55–77 and *passim*.

3. Faler, "Cultural Aspects of the Industrial Revolution"; Anthony F. C. Wallace, "A Cotton Manufacturing Village: Rockdale, Pa., 1825–1865," *Working Papers from the Regional Economic History Research Center* of the Eleutherian Mills–Hagley Foundation 1 (1977), 57–78; Robert W. Doherty, "Social Bases for the Presbyterian Schism of 1837–1838: The Philadelphia Case," *Journal of Social History* 2 (Fall 1968), 69–79; Laurie, "Nothing on Compulsion"; Leonard L. Richards, *Gentlemen of Property and Standing: Anti-Abolition Mobs in Jacksonian America* (New York, 1970), all find that revivals and their related social movements between 1826 and 1837 were strong among

a new (and primarily industrial) middle class, and among their friends in the working class. For a fine analysis of urban missions (and of their failure in an old seaport), see Rosenberg, *Religion and the Rise of the American City*. Stuart Blumin's study of Kingston, New York, offers a revealing counterpoint to the association of revivals with manufacturing. In the 1820s that city experienced rapid commercialization and the influx of huge numbers of unskilled laborers and canal men developments that might predict some sort of middle-class religious response. But there was little manufacturing activity in the town, and Blumin presents no evidence of religious revivals. See Blumin, *Urban Threshold*.

4. There is a growing body of evidence that many workingmen found their own uses for the Protestant tradition in the depression years of the late 1830s and early 1840s. (For examples, see Laurie, "Nothing on Compulsion"; Faler, "Cultural Aspects of the Industrial Revolution"; Montgomery, "The Shuttle and the Cross.") The return of revivals, the founding of new churches and of Washingtonian temperance societies, and—perhaps most of all—the strength of Millerite Adventism suggest similar developments in Rochester. The reasons why an independent working-class Protestantism arose in these years and not earlier are complex, and lie outside the boundaries of this study. But I suspect that they are bound up with the destruction of labor organizations and the weakening of the Democratic Party after 1837, and the resultant political helplessness of the working class. Works that provide the theoretical underpinnings for this hunch are cited in note 6. Note also the alternation of political and religious responses that runs throughout E. P. Thompson, *The Making of the English Working Class* (New York, 1963), esp. 388ff.

5. It is understandable that historians of the working class often view middle-class evangelicalism in these terms. Bruce Laurie, for example, suggests that employers and their ministers were consciously "adapting Protestantism to industrial capitalism" ("Nothing on Compulsion," 51). Paul Faler goes a step further and states that temperance and other revival-spawned crusades of the 1830s "had secular, not religious, origins. They derived from the pressure for greater discipline and control demanded by a competitive market economy" ("Cultural Aspects of the Industrial Revolution," 371). The problem, it seems to me, is not to separate religious from secular origins, but to define the secular origins of religion.

6. Internal divisions and the resulting political impotence of a group are major themes in the explanation of revivals and revival-like

social movements at a wide variety of places and times. The earliest, and in many ways still the clearest, statement was made by Friedrich Engels in a series of essays on early Christianity, reprinted in Karl Marx and Friedrich Engels, *On Religion* (Moscow, 1957), 316–47. See also Peter Worsley, *The Trumpet Shall Sound* (New York, 1968), and Bryan R. Wilson, *Magic and the Millennium* (New York, 1973). Wilson and Vittorio Lanternari, *The Religions of the Oppressed* (New York, 1963) include extensive bibliographies on these movements.

APPENDIX A

1. Tax records are of little help in determining the absolute wealth of individuals. Most personal property was either overlooked by assessors or hidden from them, and real estate was consistently underassessed. These problems, common to the use of tax rolls in most communities, are complicated by the fact that Rochester land was subject to wild fluctuations in value. Thus I have found it more sensible to divide taxpayers into tenths, and to speak of a man's wealth only in relation to other men in Rochester.

2. In fact, the number of shops whose owners appear in the first five deciles was much higher than can be demonstrated systematically. Many manufacturing establishments were owned by men listed with white-collar occupations. For examples among carpenters, coopers, and shoemakers, see above, 38–41.

3. This is discussed fully above, 40–41.

APPENDIX B

1. *A Catalogue of the Members of the Third Presbyterian Church in Rochester, from its Organization, Feb. 28, 1827, to Jan. 2, 1832* (Rochester, 1832).

2. Price, "Protestantism in Rochester," 279–80; Hotchkin, *Purchase and Settlement of Western New York,* 490.

3. Parsons, *History of Rochester Presbytery,* 254–55; *Charter and Directory of the City of Rochester* (Rochester, 1834), 17.

4. O'Reilley, *Settlement of the West,* 287.

5. Tryon Edwards, *Reasons for Thankfulness: A Discourse Delivered in the First Presbyterian Church in Rochester, N.Y., on the Annual Day of Thanksgiving, December 15, 1836* (Rochester, 1837), 37.

6. Price, "Protestantism in Rochester," 248ff.

7. See above, 91–92, 129, 196.

8. *Charter and Directory*, 17.

9. Rev. F. W. Conable, *History of the Genesee Annual Conference* (New York, 1876), 384–85.

10. Rev. A. H. Strong, "Historical Sketch," in *Centennial Celebration: First Baptist Church* (Rochester, 1818).

11. *Book of the First Baptist Church, Rochester, N.Y., for 1838–39* (Rochester, 1839).

12. Price, "Protestantism in Rochester," 270.

ACKNOWLEDGMENTS

This little book has been in the works for six years, and during that time I have run up innumerable debts. Samuel Friedman and Alexander Saxton have doubtless forgotten that the subject was formulated in conversations with them. Both provided encouragement and valuable suggestions throughout the early stages. Professor Saxton in particular was an endless fund of patience, encouragement, understanding, odd jobs, and sound advice. The work would not have gotten started without his help.

Many people in Rochester made my visits pleasant and productive. Without exception, ministers and secretaries at the churches provided places to work and access to their records. Special thanks are due to the Reverend David K. McMillan, then of Central Presbyterian Church. I hope I have treated his old friends with the respect that they deserve.

Most of the research was conducted in the Local History Room and the City Historian's Office at the Rochester Public Library, and in the Manuscripts and Rare Books Division of the Rush Rhees Library at the University of Rochester. At the public library, Blake McKelvey welcomed my intrusion onto his scholarly territory, showed me his city, and allowed me to pore through a closetful of his manuscript notes. Joseph Barnes, his successor as City Historian, was unfailingly generous with his time and energy. At the University of Rochester, Karl Kabelac took an early and sustained interest in the project, and went off on his own to excavate documents that proved to be of immense value. I am deeply indebted to his skilled detective work. Thanks are also due to the following libraries: UCLA, the University of California at Berkeley, the Henry E. Huntington Library, the Oberlin College Archives, the Arents Research Library at Syracuse University, the Regional History Collection at Cornell University, the Clements Library at the University of Michigan, the Legislative and Judicial Records Branch of the National Archives, the American Baptist Historical Society, and the Sterling and Beinecke Libraries at Yale University. The project required money as well as kindness, and for help in that area I am grateful to the Graduate Fellowship Office at UCLA and the A. Whitney Griswold Faculty Research Fund at Yale University.

My most immediate and lasting debts are to persons who criticized drafts of the manuscript. Writing is lonely and frustrating work, but many teachers, colleagues, and friends stepped in to ease its inevitable horrors. Stephan Thernstrom directed the dissertation from which the book has grown, and he has taken part in more conversations and read more drafts than he probably cares to remember. My debt to him is immense. Others who have helped include Nancy F. Cott, David Brion Davis, Richard W. Fox, Samuel Friedman, James A. Henretta, John R. Low-Beer, Lewis Perry, Roland Siu, Gene Walker, Sean Wilentz, and Allan M. Winkler. Special thanks to David Davis and Richard Fox, who gave the manuscript particularly thorough and penetrating critiques. In the spring of 1977 I presented some ideas for revision to faculty and graduate students at the University of Pittsburgh. The ideas, it quickly turned out, were wrong-headed. For the intelligence and good humor with which they pointed that out, I wish to thank David Montgomery, Seymour Drescher, and the others who were there. It was a rough afternoon, but I think the book is better for it.

In the final stages, Arthur Wang and Eric Foner labored heroically to improve the manuscript and to accelerate its slow-moving author. They have given sound advice, and I have stubbornly ignored much of it. Like the others who have helped, I wish to thank them without implicating them in what I have done.

Index

African Methodist Church, 117–18

Albany, N.Y., 38, 109, 137

Allcott, Simeon, 45

Andrews, Samuel G., 24

Andrews, Samuel J., 24

Andrews, Silas, 27

Andrews-Atwater Tract, 22, 24

Ann Street, 51

Anti-Masonic Enquirer, 68, 76, 126, 128

Antimasons, 20, 62–63, 66–71, 73–77, 87, 89–92, 128, 129, 130, 133

anti-Sabbatarians, 85–88, 89, 91

antislavery, 5

anxious bench, 101–2

apprentices, 39, 45, 47, 81–82

Atkinson, William, 27, 91, 92

Atwater, Caleb, 24, 25

Backus, Frederick, 22, 65, 68

bakeries, 51, 59

Bank of Rochester, 29, 64–65, 70

Bank of the United States, 133

Baptists, 44, 51, 80, 113, 121, 126, 128, 156–57; *see also individual churches*

barbers, 58

Barnard, Jehiel, 63

Barnes, Gilbert Hobbs, 5

Batavia, N.Y., 66, 67

Bath, N.Y., 23

Beach, Ebenezer, 30

Bearcup, Erastus, 54

Beecher, Lyman, 4–5, 79, 80, 83–84, 85, 92, 109

Bennett, James Gordon, 134

Berkshire County, Mass., 29

Bethel Presbyterian Church, 116–17, 154

Bethlehem, Conn., 27

Bissell, Josiah, 16, 27, 85, 91, 92–94

blacks, 40, 60, 117–18

Bloomfield, N.Y., 22, 100

boarders, 45, 46, 59, 107, 145–46

boardinghouses, 36, 39, 51, 59

boat builders, 41, 59, 120, 121

boatmen, 58, 87, 88, 116–17

Boston, Mass., 84, 109

Bowman, John, 68, 69

brickmakers, 41

Briggs, Martin, 125

Brighton, N.Y., 24, 25

Brown, David, 23

Brown, Francis, 23–24, 63

Brown, Matthew, 23–24, 31, 40, 65, 70, 79, 132

Brown, Warren, 23, 65

Brown family, 23–24, 30, 63, 73, 90

Buchan, Caroline, 99

Buchan, James, 21, 99

Bucktail Republicans, 23, 64–65, 68–71, 89, 90–91, 128, 129–30

Buffalo, N.Y., 20, 137

Buffalo Street, 31, 48, 51, 52

builders, 40–41, 44, 104, 146, 148–49
Burchard, Jedediah, 118, 119
Burnap, Ela, 127
Burned-Over District, The, 137
Bush, John, 30, 122

calkers, 120
Calvinism, 3–4, 96
Canandaigua, N.Y., 24, 25, 66, 67
carpenters, 40–41, 42, 44, 56, 59, 120, 142, 146, 148–49
Carroll, Charles, 22
Catholics, 20–21, 76, 80, 99, 128
Cavanaugh, Patrick, 74
Cayuga Bridge, N.Y., 23, 24, 25
Chapin, Moses, 65, 80
Child, Jonothan, 22, 23, 69, 79, 87, 91, 116, 128, 131–32, 143–44
Childs, Timothy, 91, 128
Christopher, John, 114
Christopher, Joseph, 114
Christopher's Mansion House, 85
Church, James, 147
Church, John, 147
circus, 53, 115
Clay, Henry, 29
clerks, 45, 47, 58, 121, 122, 123, 144
Cleveland, Ohio, 20
Clinton Street, 52
Clintonians, 63, 64–66, 67, 68, 69, 70, 71, 89, 129
clothiers, 41
Cobb, William, 63
Collins, E. W., 21
Colman, Anson, 23, 69
coopers, 40, 41–42, 120
Cornhill, 53, 131
Craftsman, The, 128
Cross, Whitney R., 137
Cuming, Rev. Francis H., 65, 68, 91

Daily Democrat, 128
Dansville, N.Y., 22
Darrow, Pierce, 40
Democrats, 20, 69, 70, 73–77, 88, 89, 129–35
Denio, John, 126, 127
Detroit, Mich., 20, 23
domestic servants, 45, 128
drinking, 44, 54, 55–61, 78, 82–83, 126–27, 130, 131
Dublin, 42, 53
Durkheim, Emile, 10–13

Eagle Tavern, 51, 54, 74
elections, 63, 73–75, 88, 130–31
Elwood, Isaac, 132
Elwood, John B., 68, 69
Ely, Elisha, 27
Ely, Harvey, 27, 40, 128
Episcopalians, 22, 30, 65, 79, 90–92, 97, 114, 116, 128, 154–55; *see also individual churches*
Erie Canal, 15, 16, 17, 54, 67, 84, 88, 94, 105–6, 114, 144
Evans, Oliver, 18
Exchange Street, 48, 53, 54, 59, 78, 125

family government, 43–48, 59
Female Charitable Society, 118
Finney, Charles G., 3–4, 5, 13–14, 15–16, 36, 38, 93–94, 95, 96–102, 103, 109–10, 140–41
Finney, Lydia, 99
First Baptist Church, 156, 158
First Methodist Church, 117, 119, 155–56
First Presbyterian Church, 44, 65, 75, 84, 87, 90, 92, 100, 113, 116, 118, 128, 152, 153, 160–61
Fitzhugh, William, 22
Fitzhugh Street, 16, 51–52, 53–54, 127
flour milling, 18–19, 30, 40, 56, 133

Ford Street, 54
forwarding merchants, 36, 105
Four Corners, 48, 53, 54
Frankfort Tract, 22, 23–24, 73
Free Presbyterian Church, 118, 119, 153
freethought, 120–21
Freewill Baptists, 117

gambling, 54, 72
Gardiner, Addison, 69, 133
Genesee Valley, 17–22, 24–25, 35–36
geographic mobility, 27, 32–34, 71, 122, 147–48, 158–61
Gibson, Rachel, 39
Gould, Jacob, 65, 70, 75
Graves, Jacob, 45
grocers, 36, 54, 60, 77–78, 105, 117, 143
grocery licenses, 58–59, 75–76, 77–78, 82, 130, 131–32

Hall, Basil, 51
Hart, Thomas, 29
Hartford, Conn., 27, 117
Hatch, Jesse, 39
hatters, 31, 41
Hawley, Jesse, 128
Hawley, Silas, 41
Hill, Charles J., 27
Hitchcock, Aaron, 78
hotelkeepers, 36, 105–6
Howell, William, 121
households, 6–7, 43–48, 52, 57–58, 106–9
Hundred-Acre Tract, 22, 64

interdenominationalism, 100–2, 109, 112, 118–19, 128, 129–30
Irish immigrants, 20–21, 42, 128

Jackson, Andrew, 133
James, Rev. William, 92–93, 111
Johnson, Elisha, 88, 91

Johnson, Sen. Richard M., 86–87
journeymen, 36–42, 144–50

Kearney, Patrick, 21
Kempshall, Thomas, 28, 30–32, 34, 122
Kempshall, Timothy, 31
Kempshall, Willis, 30, 31
King, Bradford, 40, 99–100
King, Moses, 40

labor discipline, 6, 41–42, 57, 80–83, 121–28
laborers, 36, 37, 38, 46, 56, 58, 59, 123, 133
Lafayette, Marquis de, 67
land speculators, 22–25, 28, 34, 73
lastmakers, 41
lawyers, 52, 105, 106, 143, 144
Leavitt, A. V. T., 27
Lenox, Mass., 24
Leonard, Hamilton, 21
Leroy, N.Y., 68
Livingston County, N.Y., 25
Lockport, N.Y., 137
Lynch, Peter, 21
Lyon, Isaac, 112

McIlvaine, Rev. Charles, 91–92
Mack, Daniel, 63
McKay, John, 23
McNamara, Father, 80
Main Street, 24, 52
Marshall, Elihu H., 87
Maryland, 22, 65, 70
Masonic Lodge, 29, 30, 62, 66, 67–71, 89–92, 100, 128, 129
Mechanic Street, 39, 53
merchant capitalism, 39–42, 46
metal workers, 41
Methodists, 30, 31, 76, 80, 113, 117–18, 155–56; see also individual churches
Michigan, 109
millennialism, 3–4, 109–13, 140–41

Monroe County, N.Y., 69
Monroe County Bible Society, 92
Monroe County Temperance Society, 133
Montgomery, Harvey, 23
Montreal, 17
Morgan, Edward, 54
Morgan, William, 66–67, 90, 128
Mumford, Silas, 24, 25
Mumford, Thomas, 23
Mumford, William, 24, 25

Needham, S. P., 114
New Haven, Conn., 24, 29, 32
New Measures, 97–102, 108
New York City, 18, 19, 109
Norton, Heman, 87
Noyes, John Humphrey, 110

occupational mobility, 28–32, 32–33, 122–28
Ohio, 109
Onderdonck, Rev. H. U., 91
O'Reilley, Henry, 20, 70
Othello, 54

Paine, Thomas, 120–21
paint mixers, 41
panic of 1837, 21
Parma, N.Y., 123.
Parsons, Lauren, 124
partnerships, 21–27, 34–35, 124–25
Peck, Everard, 27, 30, 43–44, 45, 63, 98, 99, 114
Peck, Jesse, 31, 43
peg makers, 41
Penfield, N.Y., 23, 24, 25
Penney, Rev. Joseph, 84, 92–93, 113
People's Party, 65, 70
Perkins, Artemissia, 101
persistence, 71, 122, 147–48, 158–61

Philadelphia, 38, 109
Piersons, James, 39
Pioneer Line, 85–87, 88, 91, 92
Pittsfield, Mass., 27, 29, 31, 32, 94
Porter, Samuel D., 99
prayer, 96–102, 109
prayer meetings, 100–1
Presbyterians, 3–4, 44, 65, 75, 80, 87, 90, 91, 92–94, 95, 97, 99, 100, 114–15, 116–17, 117–18, 128, 152–54; see also individual churches
Presbyterian General Assembly, 109
Princeton Seminary, 91
printers, 31, 43, 46, 56

Quakers, 51, 86–87

Reformed Presbyterian Church, 153–54
revivals, 3–14, 95–128
Reynolds, Abelard, 27, 28–30, 31–32, 34, 68
Reynolds Arcade, 31, 52
Rochester, John B., 69
Rochester, Nathaniel, 22–23, 25, 29, 32, 41, 63–65, 66, 68–69, 70, 79, 90, 144
Rochester, Thomas Hart, 23, 65, 91
Rochester, William B., 23, 64, 69
Rochester family, 29, 32, 70, 73, 79
Rochester Gem, 126
Rochester House, 85
Rochester Observer, 77, 80, 86, 87–88, 92, 99, 103
Rochester Savings Bank, 118
Rochester Society for the Promotion of Temperance, 79–82
Rochester Woolen Mills, 112, 122
Rome, N.Y., 23, 63
Rossiter & Knox, 114

Sabbatarians, 74–75, 83–88, 89–94, 129
Sabbath observance, 72–73, 84, 112
Sage, Oren, 51–52
St. Luke's Episcopal Church, 30, 65, 87, 90–91, 92, 97–98, 118, 128, 154, 158
St. Paul's Episcopal Church, 91–92, 100, 129, 154–55
St. Paul Street, 24, 52–53, 60, 73
Salem, Mass., 26–27
Samson, Ashley, 75
sashmakers, 41, 46
schoolteachers, 58, 59, 144
Scotch Dry Goods Store, 21
Scrantom, Edwin, 56, 76, 126, 128
Scrantom, Hamlet, 63
Scrantom family, 125
Second Baptist Church, 116–17, 157, 158
Second (Brick) Presbyterian Church, 44, 92, 99, 101, 110–12, 118, 119, 125, 126, 127, 152, 160–61
Sellig, Andrew, 78
Selye, Lewis, 121–22, 125, 126, 127
Seymour, James, 68, 70
Sheldon, Thomas, 69
Shepard, Erastus, 126
shoe binders, 39
shoemakers, 38–40, 42, 46–47, 56, 104, 120, 142
Six Sermons on Intemperance, 80
Smith, Albert, 113–14
Smith, E. Darwin, 128
Smith, Elijah, 113–14
Smith, Melania, 98–99
Sophia Street, 52, 54
Sprague brothers, 115
Spring Street, 23
Stanton, Henry B., 76
State Street, 31, 48, 54

Stevens, Hestor L., 132, 133
Stevens, John C., 59
Steward, Austin, 117–18
Stone, Alvah, 24, 25
Stone, Enos Sr., 24
Stone, Enos Jr., 22, 24, 25, 29
Stone, Orange, 24, 25
stonemasons, 120
strikes, 42, 120
Strong, Alvah, 125–26, 127, 128, 129
Strong, J. W., 63, 65
Strong, King, 29
Strong, Mary, 31
Strong family, 70, 73
Sunday schools, 111
Susquehanna River, 17, 22

tailors, 41
tanneries, 45, 53
Tappan, Lewis, 85
teamsters, 58
temperance, 55, 60–61, 75, 78, 79–84, 87, 89, 90, 94, 113–14, 121–22, 126–27, 129, 130–33
theater, 54, 58, 76, 77
Third Presbyterian Church, 3–4, 85, 92, 117, 152
tinsmiths, 46
Tocqueville, Alexis de, 9, 32–33, 84, 136–37, 138–39
tramping journeymen, 120
Troup Street, 54
Tucker, Luther, 40, 69

Utica, N.Y., 109, 137

Van Buren, Martin, 64, 68, 69
Vermont, 109

Ward, Levi, 65, 79
Ward family, 70, 73, 90
Water Street, 53, 78
Weed, Thurlow, 64, 66, 67, 68, 69, 74, 75–76

214   INDEX

Weld, Theodore Dwight, 113–14
Wells, Eliphalet, 28
West, Ira, 30, 32
Whig Party, 7–8, 128–35
Whitehouse, Rev. Henry J., 97–98
Whittlesey, Frederick, 24, 74, 76, 78, 91, 128
Whittlesey, William, 24
Wilberforce Colony, 117

Willson, Robert, 44
Wilson, Jane, 111
Windsor, Conn., 28
Wisner, Rev. William, 112
women and revivals, 7, 57–58, 98–99, 107–8, 118
Works, Samuel, 45

Young Men's Temperance Society, 133